LANDMARK COLLECTOR'S LIBRARY

Lost Buildings
around
Nantwich

ANDREW LAMBERTON AND ROBIN GRAY

DEDICATION

This book is dedicated to Robin Gray
who sadly died during the course of its preparation.
Robin was keen to ensure that items of historical interest were not
lost to future generations. With his love of the countryside, a deeply engrained
knowledge of Nantwich and its surrounding area, an appreciation of its
history, and the many friends he made there, it has enabled us to
produce a unique volume which is a fitting
tribute to his memory.

LANDMARK COLLECTOR'S LIBRARY

LOST BUILDINGS
AROUND
NANTWICH

ANDREW LAMBERTON AND ROBIN GRAY

Landmark Publishing

Published by

Landmark Publishing Ltd
Ashbourne Hall, Cokayne Ave, Ashbourne, Derbyshire DE6 1EJ England
Tel: (01335) 347349 Fax: (01335) 347303
e-mail: landmark@clara.net
website: www.landmarkpublishing.co.uk

ISBN 13: 978-1-84306-229-5

ISBN 10: 1-84306-229-1

© Andrew Lamberton & Robin Gray 2006

The rights of the authors to this work has
been asserted by them in accordance with the Copyright,
Design and Patents Act, 1993.

All rights reserved. No part of this publication may be reproduced, stored in a retrieval
system or transmitted in any form or by any means, electronic, mechanical, photocopying,
recording or otherwise without the prior permission of Landmark Publishing Ltd.
For the avoidance of doubt, this includes reproduction of any
image in this book on an internet site.

British Library Cataloguing in Publication Data: a catalogue
record for this book is available from the British Library.

Print: Cromwell Press Ltd, Trowbridge
Design: Mark Titterton

Front cover: Ashbrook Towers
Title page: An early photograph of Calveley Hall.
Back cover top: Griffiths' Cottage, Bluestone
Back cover bottom left: Wells Green Farmhouse
Back cover bottom right: Hawke's Cottage, Edleston

CONTENTS

ACKNOWLEDGEMENTS	6
INTRODUCTION	7
SECTION 1 NORTH EAST	**8**
Woolstanwood	10
Wistaston	11
Rope	22
Willaston	23
Shavington	26
SECTION 2 SOUTH EAST	**31**
Stapeley	33
Batherton	41
Wybunbury	43
Walgherton	49
Lea	52
Blakenhall	54
Checkley	54
Doddington	54
Bridgemere	57
Hunsterson	58
Hatherton	59
Hankelow	62
SECTION 3 SOUTH WEST	**63**
Austerson	65
Coole Pilate	71
Baddington	73
Edleston	73
Sound	75
Ravensmoor	76
Newhall	77
Wrenbury	87
Baddiley	100
Acton	101
Burland	106
Chorley	107
SECTION 4 NORTH WEST	**108**
Brindley	110
Faddiley	110
Reaseheath	111
Worleston	112
Hurleston	114
Poole	115
Stoke	116
Wardle	117
Calveley	119
Aston juxta Mondrum	121
Church Minshull	122
APPENDIX	
Nantwich Lost Houses	132
BIBLIOGRAPHY	**138**
INDEX	**139**

ACKNOWLEDGEMENTS

Thanks are due to Judy St Pourcain for her help in research for this book, to Melvyn Reynolds for producing the maps and Kevin Greener for the transfer of all the many photographs to disc.

We are grateful to The National Monuments Record at English Heritage for permission to use photographs in their possession, to the staff at the Cheshire Record Office for their assistance in research, Nantwich Library and The Nantwich Chronicle.

Several people have been extremely helpful in supplying information and pictures of their own locality and these include Frank Cheetham, Peter Bebbington, Janet Gray, Geoff Maddocks, and Orville Kelly. Particular thanks also go to Frank Williams for his information and photographs concerning RAF Hack Green. Thanks also go to the following who have provided information and/or photographs: Peter Clough, Nancy Dutton, Reg and Barbara Baker, Anne and David Owen, Jill and David Alexander, Emily Pace, Jean Clough, Mrs Blacklay, Elaine Joynson and Alan Jones, Bernice Lamberton, Jeremy and Sally Bevan, Elizabeth Bull, Joan Smith, Hilda Mottram, Arthur Griffiths, John Parker, Richard and Tony Sadler, Harold and Mrs Owen, Derek Hughes, Roy Cope, Derek Brookshaw, Gwen and Albert Goldstraw, Mr and Mrs John Roach, Ann and David Jones, Dan and David Freedman, Mike Blackburn, May Griffiths, Harry Ikin, David Clarke, Gwen Laganowski, Ian Bennion, Mrs Dakin, Lilian Parker, Peter Cooke, Brian Moore, Janet Spibey, Margaret Sandlands, Gillian Stewart, Tony Cleaver, Terry Wynne and Helen Cope. To Andrew Griffin for his permission to use the photograph of Berkeley Towers.

To Pauline Crump of P. Williams, Chemist for assistance in photographic reproduction, and Mark and Julie Simon of The Paper Place for copying facilities. Finally to Steve Lawson and his staff at Nantwich Bookshop.

Introduction

During the preparation of this book, Robin very sadly passed away, but his contribution was such that it was felt important for his name to be retained as co-author. Indeed this book includes many buildings of which Robin had a personal knowledge.

This volume follows on from the previous book *Lost Houses in Nantwich* published in 2005 and covers an area around Nantwich with almost 40 parishes (it should be noted that not every parish in the locality is included). It is divided into four sections which represent the four quadrants of the compass and the reader is taken in a clockwise direction around Nantwich starting in the north-east and finishing in the north-west. The outer limits of this survey are somewhat loose and are dependent on the author's own knowledge of the locality. It was decided to cover the Nantwich rural area and not to include urban areas such as the town of Crewe in this survey, and in fact the Wistaston section goes no nearer to Crewe than Wistaston brook.

The use of early maps has been invaluable. The enclosed maps of Bryant in 1831 have proved a good starting point but also appropriate Tithe maps (and there were many) have been referred to, together with the later OS 1st Edition maps of *c.*1875 and the 3rd Edition maps of *c.*1910.

A variety of age and style of building is covered and while the emphasis is on domestic dwellings, other buildings of interest have been included. To mention a few: the several rebuilds of St Chad's church, Wybunbury; a cheese factory where Robin worked for over forty years; two RAF bases, one a radar station, the other an aerodrome; a large military encampment with over 100 buildings built during the Second World War; water mills including a leather mill; a dyer's mill; a paper mill; a bone mill; and a wooden railway halt.

There are really only three grand houses included, namely Calveley Hall, Ashbrook Towers and Woodhey Hall, and so the emphasis is placed on smaller property – but some would say equally as important as it reflects a greater cross-section of the community.

The definition of 'lost' has proved somewhat loose and a few buildings are in fact still standing but in such derelict condition that it is considered that they will disappear in the near future. There is, however, one excellent example in this book of a building of considerable architectural interest which was rescued in a derelict condition, dismantled, and re-erected on a new site elsewhere. This is Austerson Old Hall, and while not strictly lost, it is lost to the immediate area. Also there are various buildings which have only recently been identified as being public houses at some time in the past. This book is in no way considered to be a comprehensive list of vanished buildings and there are many modernised and rebuilt rural houses which have inevitably escaped attention. It was decided not to include mediaeval moated sites as they are well documented elsewhere apart from one, Cheney Hall, Willaston, whose site was destroyed when the Nantwich Bypass was built *c.*1990.

There has been considerable recent interest in some houses scheduled for demolition in suburban surroundings. This unfortunate trend in recent years has allowed perfectly habitable and soundly built houses standing in quite large gardens to be razed to the ground so that a housing development of several dwellings can be squeezed onto that same site. In some cases there have been significant demonstrations from the local community and representations from national organisations, sadly all to no avail. A few examples are included in this book.

Finally, an appendix at the end of the book incorporates photographs and one pen and ink drawing of Nantwich houses which have come to light since the publication of the previous volume, *Lost Houses in Nantwich*.

Section 1

NORTH-EAST

North-East

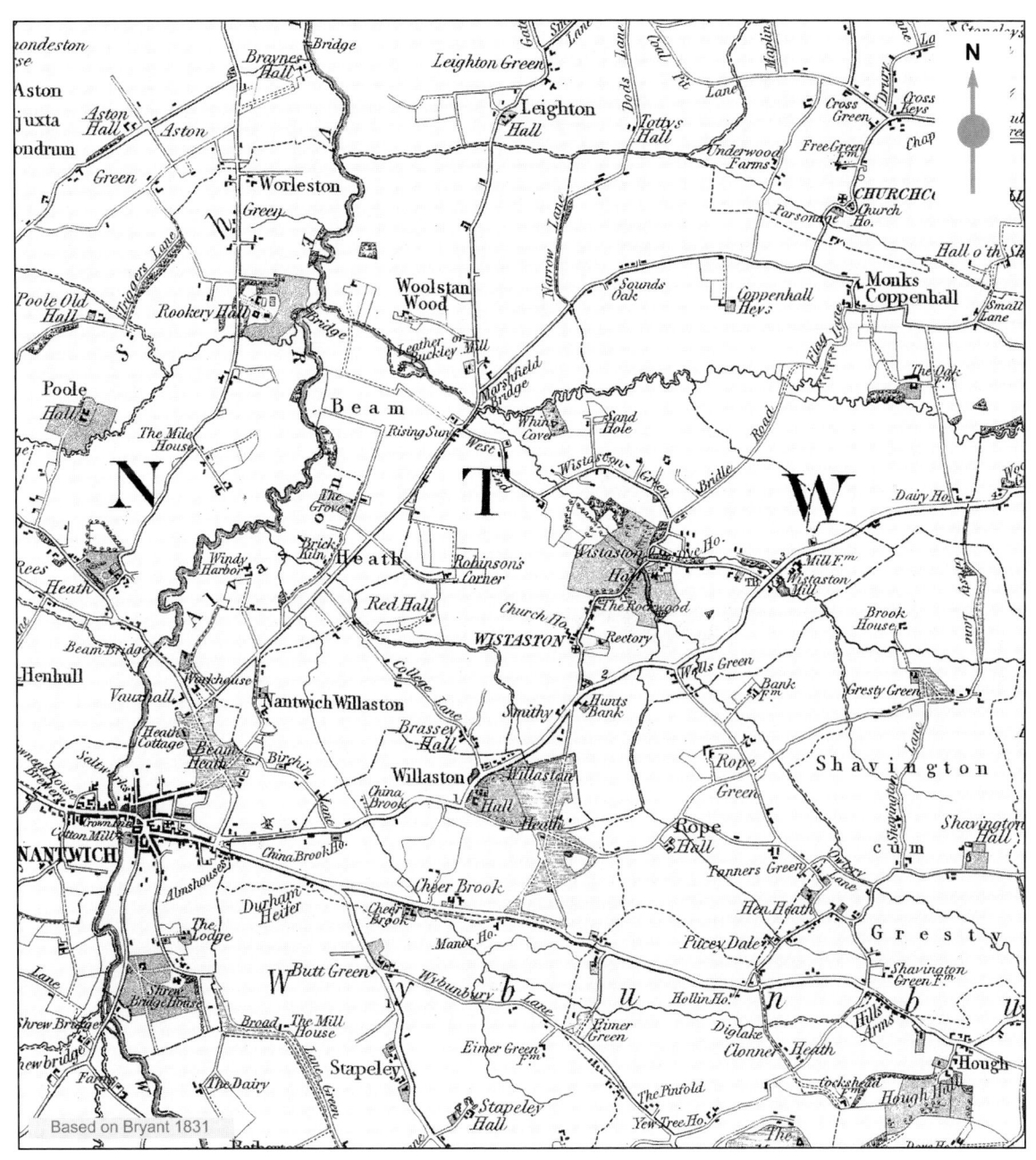

WOOLSTANWOOD

Buckley Mill

As one travels towards Crewe on the Middlewich Road out of Nantwich, just opposite the Rising Sun is a lane which leads to Buckley Mill. The mill no longer exists but a modern house now occupies part of the site. The name arises from the ownership of the mill in mediaeval times by the Bulkeley family. According to James Hall in his *History of Nantwich* written in 1883, 'the capital messuage and mill' was owned by the Griffins of Batherton during Henry VIII's reign, from whom it was purchased by Sir Henry Delves of Doddington prior to 1666. The estate was later sold to Thomas Wickstead Esq. of Townwell House, Nantwich early in the ninteenth century.

The Bryant Map of 1831 refers to the mill as Buckley or Leather Mill. It is thought that the reference to leather may have been to the fact that the oak bark used in the tanning industry had to be ground into a fine powder and this process could well have been carried out here using the same grindstones as those used for flour.

The 1838 Tithe Map for Woolstanwood shows the mill butting up to the water (known as Valley Brook) with another building, probably a storehouse, to the west and parallel to the mill. The c.1875 OS 1st Edition map names the mill as Buckley Mill (flour) and shows it this time straddling the water with another separate building behind the mill. On the c.1910 OS 3rd Edition map the mill is no longer standing and the separate storehouse has been converted into living accommodation some time previously.

It is known that Baron von Schroeder of Rookery Hall had acquired the property and land in the late nineteenth century and had made a road from Rookery Hall to the Middlewich Road across this land passing close to the mill site. This road was used as a short cut for the Baron when he wanted to use Crewe Station. He had a lodge built near the mill site which was only demolished in the 1990s when the present owner of the site had the new house built.

Buckley Mill Lodge, Woolstanwood. It is thought to have been built by Baron Schroeder on his short cut to Crewe Station from Rookery Hall, Worleston.

Harold Norris wrote an article entitled 'The Water Powered Corn Mills of Cheshire', in *Transactions of the Lancashire and Cheshire Antiquarian Society* of 1965/6 and reported that the mill was probably undershot with one wheel. He added that the building, i.e. Buckley Mill Cottage, had recently been demolished and that its position indicated a storehouse or something similar.

The earliest record so far found of a miller at Buckley Mill is in the 1851 Census where William Lindop, miller, aged 38 is listed with his wife Ann née Stretch, miller's wife aged 36, with 3 sons, William Henry aged 7, John aged 6, and Richard James aged 1. Also living there was a servant, Samuel Timmis, miller's labourer aged 16. In 1861, William is described as miller and farmer of 27 acres and he had four more sons: George aged 9, Alfred aged 7, Albert aged 2 and Levi William aged 1. Some time after this, the family moved away because the miller in 1871 was Henry Lea. Henry later moved to Wistaston Mill and apparently took the mill wheel and some machinery with him. There is also information from a Sarah Annie Lea who was born at Buckley Mill in 1880. Her father was James Thomas Lea (from Wistaston Mill) and the family later moved to Sandbach Mill.

Marshfield Gate Tollhouse

Right on the junction of the fork to Crewe at Marshfield Bank was built a tollhouse with gate on the Nantwich to Middlewich Road by the Nantwich Middlewich Turnpike Trust, probably some time in the early nineteenth century. It can be seen clearly on the Tithe Map of Woolstanwood in 1838 and also on the *c*.1875 OS 1st Edition map. It may also have controlled the road into Crewe as well. It is unclear when the building was demolished. There is a gravestone in Baddiley churchyard recording the death of William Barker of Middlewich Gate, Marshfield Bank, aged 64 in 1885 who must have been the toll keeper here.

Woolstanwood Methodist Chapel

In 1870, a chapel was built at the top of Marshfield Bank in connection with the Crewe Wesleyan Circuit. This building was erected to accommodate meetings and services which had previously been held by a small group of worshippers at Marshfield Bank Farm from 1830 onwards. This chapel provided services for local Methodists right up until its closure in 1969. It was subsequently sold in 1972 for just £200 and later demolished. A modern house now stands on its site.

WISTASTON

The Old Rectory

The present Rectory in Wistaston is a recent replacement of an earlier building not quite on the same site but still opposite and quite near to the church. In 1839 it was described as the Glebe House and in 1850 the earlier building was described as being near the east end of the church and almost completely rebuilt by the present rector, who was at that time the Rev. Thomas Brooke. Norman Robinson, writing in the 1993 *Roundabout* magazine for Wistaston people, remembers the Wistaston School Garden Party held here every summer. There were treasure hunts in the garden, followed by strawberries and cream and finally dancing on the lawn. Rector Walter Mayne officiated the proceedings with assistance from the Headmaster, Mr Platt, and schoolteachers Misses Evanson, Watson and Evans.

Lost Buildings around Nantwich

Above: Thatched black and white cottages in Church Lane, Wistaston. The one on the left still stands (with a different roof) but the building on the right has gone.

Left: This black and white thatched building is the one on the right of the previous photograph. It was a public house called The Rockwood at one time.

The Rockwood Inn, Church Lane

Opposite No. 61, Church Lane stood a black and white building quite near the road. On the enclosed Bryant Map of 1831, the building is marked as The Rockwood. Dr A.J. MacGregor in *The Alehouses and Alehouse-keepers of Cheshire 1692–1829* published in 1992 suggests that this public house was named after a well-known greyhound. He also gives the names of the licensees of The Dog, as it then was called. They were, from 1765 to 1817, John Profit and from 1818 to 1828, John Dale. It was still a public house in 1839. In 1850, John Fisher is listed as victualler and shopkeeper and in 1860 he is listed as victualler of the Rockwood Inn. In 1864 William Powell is listed as proprietor of the Dog Inn. It was closed some time after this when the owner of Wistaston Hall objected to the noise of drunks keeping him awake at night. The building became two cottages which were eventually demolished around 1960.

Also nearer the church on the same side of the road there is a Sunday School shown on the 1839 Tithe Map.

A later view of the black and white building that was at one time The Rockwood Inn.

Boote's Dye Mill

In *Wistaston, a history of the Parish and Church,* published in 1960, Norman Sedgwick refers to the Manorial mill associated with Wistaston Hall and on the right bank of Wistaston Brook in the vicinity of the Hall. Its location is opposite Wistaston Park immediately to the north of Wistaston Brook. Apparently, it was a dyer's mill but described as a freehold house in 1835 in the possession of Richard Boote, dyer. He is listed here in 1850 but by 1860 he had gone. The mill foundations were still remembered by Wistaston folk in the 1930s. It is shown quite clearly on the 1839 Tithe Map with an access road from Valley Road to the south of where the Woodside Public House is now.

Shop, Wistaston Park, Broughton Lane

A single-storey building selling greengroceries for many years between Wistaston Cottage and Wistaston Park may well be the same building that Robinson refers to as Bunce's Café. A modern house now stands on the site.

Yew Tree Farm, Broughton Lane

A most interesting black and white farmhouse called Yew Tree Farm stood in Broughton Lane not far from the present Yew Tree Drive. It is described together with a floor plan in *English Vernacular Houses* written in 1975 by Eric Mercer. It is thought to have been built in the second half of the seventeenth century, and originally consisted of two rooms with a

Yew Tree Farm, Broughton Lane, Wistaston, painted by the former vicar of Christchurch, the Reverend Stephens. It stood near to what is now Yew Tree Drive.

The front of Yew Tree Farm in the 1940s.

central fireplace with the hall to the north. There were later extensions to the north, south and east.

In 1839, Samuel Basford lived here, in 1874 it was William Dobson Adams, and in 1914 George Robinson was the tenant.

Robinson gives a brief history of the farm and estate. Apparently the farm gate was a few yards south of Yew Tree Drive and one of the two yew trees which stood each side of the gate still stands in the garden of No. 11a Broughton Lane. It seems that his grandfather, George Robinson, bought the farm and surrounding fields from the Wistaston Hall Estate when it was sold off in 1919. His father took over the farm on the death of his grandfather and continued there until the farm and estate were sold for housing in the 1960s.

Yew Tree Villa, Broughton Lane

Opposite Yew Tree Farm on the north side of Broughton Lane stood a smallholding called Yew Tree Villa. In 1839, Charles Whittingham lived here and in 1892, John Bebbington. In 1914 it was John Tatton and in 1939 it was Mrs Mary Tatton. A yew tree still stands on this side of the road, marking the site of the farm. The farm was presumably demolished some time in the 1960s.

Wistaston Gate Tollhouse, Nantwich Road

On the corner of Broughton Lane and Nantwich Road stood a tollhouse with tollgate that was built for the Nantwich to Wheelock Turnpike Trust. It jutted out into the road and had windows so that traffic could be easily seen in both directions. A white bungalow stands on the site but is situated somewhat further back from the road than the tollhouse.

In 1835, the tollhouse keeper was William Mottram, in 1839 John Rushton and in 1861 the occupants of Nantwich Road Toll Bar were James Heard, aged 38, shoemaker and his wife, Jane, aged 33, toll collector. It is assumed that the toll gate ceased to function around 1875 when the Turnpike Trusts were wound up and the responsibility of road upkeep was transferred to the newly formed County Council. It may have later been used as a shop because in 1914 Henry Lea, who later took over Wistaston Mill from his uncle, is listed here as a shopkeeper.

Wistaston Mill

Although still standing, Wistaston Mill is thought to be worthy of inclusion because it is one of the few mills in the area to survive relatively intact and is therefore an excellent example of what a typical mill used to be like. Having said that, each individual mill was unique as it had to fit into its existing and surrounding landscape. No two mills are alike.

The mill itself was in use until 1966 when the bearings failed on the overshot wheel and it had been in the possession of the well-known milling family of Lea for at least 100 years. William Wright is listed in 1839 and 1850 as the miller here.

Mollie Lea gives an interesting and valuable insight into the history and workings of the mill in *Cheshire Genealogist* magazine, Spring 1996.

The mill has been sensitively converted into a private house. There is still one set of stones intact existing as a feature in the living room and one mill wheel can be seen through a glass window set in the floor. Most of the original mill machinery is intact and still in remarkably good condition in the mill building itself.

The mill pool has now disappeared.

Rear view of Wistaston Mill. This has now been converted to a private house and the millpool has gone.

Another view of Wistaston Mill, the mill pool was just to the right of this picture.

The front of Wistaston Mill in the 1960s.

Berkeley Towers

This large private house was built in 1892 by Alfred Silvester Day. In his booklet *Berkeley Towers Crewe – A Short History*, published in 1993, Andrew Griffin covers 100 years of its history. Apparently it had eight rooms on the ground floor, six rooms upstairs, two cellars and three staircases. The outbuildings were originally used as stables. There was a stone carving on the balcony at the front of the house with the initials of Alfred Silvester Day and the date 1892 and above, the motto "Facta non Verba", meaning "deeds not words". The grounds extended to over two acres. Griffin reports that:

"The most impressive of all the rooms is the present day (1993) boardroom covering three hundred square feet. It was once thought that this was a private chapel but recent research shows that it was originally designed as a music room. With a wood block floor, dark oak panelling to a height of nine feet gives way to a series of murals depicting music through the ages and around the world in a style drawing heavily on William Morris. Tucked away almost at ceiling height are individual carvings of the Nightingale, Lark, Song Thrush, and Blackbird. An open fireplace stands at one end of the room opposite where once stood a pipe organ. The panelling around the room conceals seven cupboards ... A stained glass window carries the motif of a Cheshire sheaf of corn and the Staffordshire knot together with the phrases 'Utile Dulci' – 'Useful and Agreeable' and 'Ars longa' – 'Art is Long' (an abbreviation of 'Ars Longa Vita Brevis' – 'Art is Long, Life is Short'). Also seen in the window are the national emblems of Red Roses, Thistles, a Shamrock and a Leek. Surrounding these features red and green flowers represent a window box."

The house remained in private ownership until 1942 after which it was bought by The Ministry of Works which then led to it being used as offices for the Ministry of Agriculture Fisheries and Food. To allow for expansion, two rows of offices were built behind the house in 1948 followed by a third row in 1959. In the 1970s the whole site was refurbished, but apparently there was little alteration to the house interior.

The buildings continued to be used by the MAAF until August 1998 when they moved to a new site on the Crewe Gates Industrial Estate. Berkeley Towers then remained empty until demolition *c*.2005.

An early postcard showing Berkeley Towers, Wistaston.

Wells Green Farmhouse

This building has had a long and interesting history. It is more than unfortunate that it was demolished despite strong objections from many local residents who had formed The Wells Green Action Group. Although strong arguments were put forward for its retention on historical grounds of national importance, Wistaston has lost yet another landmark building in a central location. Sedgwick gives quite a comprehensive coverage of its history but it is worth mentioning some of the important points. There is no doubt that the original building was timber framed and erected around the end of the sixteenth century. The house contained beams of 'Kings' Oak' of great length, running the full length of the building. Their length and age suggest that they may predate the Armada, and they had carpenters' marks on them of Roman numerals. The staircase and gallery landing were also made from oak and there were examples of wattle and daub walls in the attic and on the ground floor.

Wells Green Farmhouse, immediately prior to demolition. Strong objections by the local community to demolition were unsuccessful.

Wells Green Farmhouse before removal of trees and shrubs.

The house is thought to have been built by the Minshull family and it was Elizabeth Minshull who became the poet John Milton's third wife in 1663. It is thought that he may have lived there for about 18 months.

The building was encased in local hand-made brick in the 1830s but the layout was basically left unaltered.

In 1951, the building was divided into two halves by Mrs Barnes, whose family then lived in the left-hand half, becoming known as No. 4 Rope Lane. The Barnes family lived here until 1985, followed by Mr and Mrs Herringe from 1986 to 1996. At No. 2 Rope Lane, the Hodgson family lived here from 1954 for about 20 years followed by Mr and Mrs Fox from 1977 to 1986.

As mentioned above, despite the strong feelings of many locals, the action was unsuccessful and the house was demolished in the spring of 2006.

Spar Shop, Rope Lane

This building was originally a barn belonging to Wells Green farmhouse. Mr Hodgson used the front part as a garage in the 1950s and 1960s and the back half was used for the poultry business of the Barnes family. This developed into a frozen food outlet for Barnes and Green using the whole of the building. This later became a general store and Spar shop including a post office. This building was also demolished with Wells Green Farmhouse in the spring of 2006, and a larger two-storey replacement building erected behind.

Spar Shop and Post Office, Wells Green, prior to demolition. This building was originally a barn belonging to Wells Green Farmhouse.

North-East

320, Crewe Road

This building is due for demolition at the time of writing. Despite strong opposition from local residents, the local parish councils, English Nature and the Council for the Protection of Rural England, plans for demolition have been approved.

320, Crewe Road, Wistaston. This house was due for demolition in 2006, to be replaced by a small housing estate on its land.

The Horse and Jockey

Although it is impossible to locate exactly where this licensed alehouse stood in Wistaston, there is a possibility that it may be connected with local horse racing in the locality at the time. According to MacGregor, its licence ran from 1779 to 1788 and the licensee was Francis Ryley. It is recorded that horse races were held annually on Beam Heath land for two to three days in June and July from 1729 until the land was sold in 1824 but the exact location of the course was unknown until recently. The land was ploughed when sold and all trace of the course was lost. However, the enclosed section of the Greenwood Map of 1819 shows the circuit quite clearly and it crosses the Nantwich to Middlewich road in two places. It is thought that the alehouse could well have been on that same road and close to the raceground.

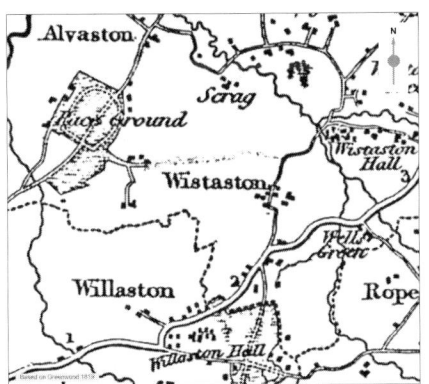

ROPE

Rope Bank Farm

A farm has existed at Rope Bank since around the 1820s. It later came into the possession of the Young family. It ceased to be a farm in the late 1960s when the surrounding farmland was sold for building development. The farmhouse, however, still survived as a private house and Mr Smith, the local solicitor, lived here for some time. The outbuildings were converted into a separate private dwelling around 1990. The house is completely surrounded by the large housing estate and has now (2006) been sold for demolition and building development.

The front of Rope Bank Farm immediately prior to demolition.

The rear of Rope Bank Farm. The two wings were later additions.

Rope Bridge Farm

A more recent farm was built at Rope Bridge some time after the railway was built around 1855. However, the farmhouse did not survive long and is thought to have been demolished around the mid-1950s. The outbuildings, however, survived and were converted into living accommodation in the 1960s.

WILLASTON

The Barracks, Coppice Road

The *c.*1875 1st Edition OS map shows Coppice Road to have been named Barracks Lane. There is no other evidence of such a building existing in Coppice Road.

46, Wistaston Road

A large white house stood back from the road at the junction of Wistaston Road and Coppice Road (known locally as Stores Corner after the Co-op Stores that was situated on the opposite side of the road on the corner). Rowlands' hairdressing business operated from here just before demolition around 1999. Three houses now stand on this site.

Wistaston Road, Willaston, showing No. 46, the white house, and beyond, the Primitive Methodist Chapel, both of which have been demolished.

Primitive Methodist Chapel, Wistaston Road

This chapel was built in 1875 and was part of the Crewe circuit. It closed in the mid-1960s. The minister in 1914 was Rev. C. Finlay. The separate Sunday school was advertised in 1914 as a lecture hall with facilities for public lectures, entertainments, social evenings, etc. The buildings were demolished in the late 1960s and now four houses occupy the site.

Willaston Fire Station, Wistaston Road

There is a reference to this building in 1914. Willaston Fire Brigade consisted then of Captain A. Forster, Sergeants J. Noden and J. Chapman and Firemen G. Whalley, T. Lightfoot, J. Holt, J. Done, J. Noden, jnr, R. Owen and T. Jones. The alarm of fire was given at the fire station by a bell. The most likely site for this building would be at the corner of Trickett's Lane and Wistaston Road. A garage and coal yard were situated here at a later date. Now Trickett's Mews are here.

Park Mills Clothing Factory

The c.1910 3rd Edition OS map shows the clothing factory to be in existence then. In 1914 and 1939, the owners were listed as Joseph Crook and Sons. It may have been used for velvet cutting in 1914. It was later taken over by Kindlers, whose manager was Mr Posna, and finally Lewings, before closing around the year 2000.

The Mission Church, Park Road

A small wooden hut in Shufflebotham's orchard was used for many years for church services in Willaston. This was an outreach church from St Mary's, Wistaston. Around the mid-1970s, the land it was on was sold for development and a larger building was erected in Coppice Road which is called St Luke's and used for regular church services.

Cheney Hall, Mediaeval Moated Site

The mediaeval moated site of Cheney Hall was largely removed by the construction of the Nantwich Bypass in 1989. It was situated to the south-east of the Willaston Board School. An excavation of the site was carried out immediately prior to the road construction and this revealed the remains of a large timber drawbridge that once spanned the moat. Such finds are fairly uncommon. Several of the larger timbers carried carpenters' marks and were chamfered and bevelled. Carbon dating revealed that the timbers were felled some time after 1215 and before the end of the fourteenth century. The wooden building on the site is thought to have been the home of William Cheney from at least 1316 and was abandoned possibly as late as 1700.

The Peacock Inn, Crewe Road

The original Peacock Inn still stands at the end of Brook buildings just some 100 yards nearer Nantwich than the current Peacock Hotel. A careful examination of the end wall shows that some of the lettering from the Peacock Hotel is still visible. It is not known when the licence was transferred to its present location but it is thought to have been in the 1950s. It had just one bed for visitors in 1891.

The original Peacock, Crewe Road, Willaston. It stands about 100 yards away from the present Peacock Hotel.

Cheerbrook Gate Tollhouse, Newcastle Road

A tollhouse stood here for many years and was demolished around 1990 when the Nantwich Bypass was constructed. There is a floor plan of the original house showing a living room 12ft square with a pantry behind 8ft by 4ft and two bedrooms, one 7ft by 9ft at the front and the other behind 9ft by 9ft. Windows were provided at both sides to look out for oncoming traffic. The cost of the building including the tollgate was only £90. In 1861, Henry Parry, aged 37, post office messenger, lived here with his wife Margaret, aged 41, who was the toll collector. It ceased to be a tollhouse around 1875 when the turnpike trusts were wound up and road upkeep became the responsibility of the County Council.

Many Willaston people remember Mary and Billy Wilson having a little shop here selling sweets, ice cream and lemonade with flowers and vegetables on a stall outside and open on Sundays.

Cheerbrook Tollhouse, Willaston demolished c. 1990. Many local people remember Mary and Billy Wilson who had a stall in front of the house.

22, Cheerbrook Road

The white bungalow at this address has just been demolished at the time of writing (2006) to be replaced with two houses on the same site. It is thought that the previous building was the home of The Hon. Mrs Campbell, a well-known figure in the Guiding community.

SHAVINGTON

Shavington Mill, Crewe Road

A mill was built here some time not long before 1850. There is no evidence of a building on the 1839 Tithe Map. The miller is listed as James Bourne in 1850 and in 1860 it was William Wakefield. On the c.1872 1st Edition OS map it is shown as a flour mill indicating that it was used for several types of cereal. Norris reported that there was a single overshot wheel with the water running along the length of the building and the pool was where the bowling green is now. There is an entry in a directory of 1892 that refers to William Healing miller (steam). It is not known if this refers to Shavington Mill. By c.1910, the mill had become disused and it later became the Shavington Workingmen's Social Club which it is still.

North-East

Shavington Social Club. This building used to be Shavington Mill.

The side and rear of the above building.

Farmhouse, Crewe Road

A modern house now stands on the site of a farmhouse just behind the present Shavington Doctor's Surgery. In 1839, the house buildings and yard were owned by Robert Green Hill and the tenant was George Edwards. The last farmer here was Mr Galley. This building was derelict from at least the 1960s until it was demolished some time later.

The Toc H Club, Crewe Road

This small building stood on the corner of Crewe Road and Baron's Road. It was originally built as a chapel by a branch of the Wesleyan Methodists known as the Warrenites in 1837. It was rented by the Toc H society from at least the 1950s and also used as a boys' club. It was demolished in the 1990s to make room for the present house owned by the Methodist Church to provide a home for the local minister.

Bungalow, Crewe Road

A bungalow that stood on the corner of Baron's Road and Crewe Road, opposite the Toc H Club, was demolished in the 1980s to make way for the present bungalow on the same site.

12, Crewe Road

A bungalow was built here, probably in the 1940s. It was demolished in 2005 to make way for a new dwelling.

3 and 5, Rope Lane

Two old semi-detached cottages which stood here were demolished during the 1970s and replaced by two detached houses.

Primitive Methodist Chapel, Rope Lane

This building is thought to have been built in 1830; however there is no indication of a building here on the 1839 Tithe Map. Quite probably meetings were being held locally in a private house. There is evidence that the chapel was opened in 1869. It was demolished in 1987 and a modern house now stands on this site.

Chestnut House, Rope Lane

A large old detached house called Chestnut House was built here some time after 1839. It had outbuildings including stables and had an attached paddock and orchard. Miss Trickett was the last occupant and apparently she had a large mural painted on one of the inside walls. The buildings were demolished in the 1980s and Santune House, a residential home for the elderly, has been built here.

Rose Cottage, Rope Lane

A very old cottage, probably originally thatched, stood here on a fair-sized plot. It was left derelict for a long time. The present bungalow of the same name stands on this same site.

Cottage, Main Road

A cottage stood on the site of the current Late Shop yard, next to 117, Main Road. It was demolished in the 1970s.

Shavington Old Mill, Pusey Dale

The Tithe Map of 1839 shows several fields here named as Mill Fields and also Mill Meadow. They are shown just to the north of Pusey Dale across Main Road. There is no visual evidence now of a mill here but Geoffrey Nulty in his book *Shavington – The Story of a South Cheshire Village*, written in 1959, suggests that there was a mill pool here and that Pusey is a corruption of Poolsey and hence pool. He says:

"There can, however, be little doubt of the existence of a pool. There is in the field names, much stronger evidence for a pool – in fact, a mill pool and therefore the existence of a mill. It will be noted that the Mill Fields lie to the east of Puseydale on the stream which may today be much smaller than its old English or mediaeval counterpart."

Cottage, Pusey Dale

Local people remember buying vegetables from a shop here run for many years by the Gibb family. It was demolished around the 1970s and a modern house at 63, Main Road now stands on this site.

Cottage, Main Road

A cottage used to stand in what is now the garden of 10, Main Road.

Shop, Newcastle Road

A shop stood on what is now part of the garden to 293, Newcastle Road opposite the Elephant. It was demolished around 1980.

Wolfe's Cottage, Elephant and Castle

The origin of the cottage name is uncertain. It may have been the name of a previous tenant called Wolfe. Also the Elephant and Castle was supplied by the Crewe firm of brewers called Woolfe at one time, but this derivation is thought to be more unlikely.

This cottage stood in what is now the yard of the Elephant public house. Robin was born here as it was the home of his grandparents. He provides a description of this cottage. This was a long narrow building rather unusually divided into three parts. The shippon was on the left as one faces the front, the living quarters in the middle consisting of two downstairs rooms and two bedrooms above and a stable to the right. On entering the kitchen/living room, through the front door, the kitchen range can be seen to the right. There is a window on each side of the front door, and surprisingly there were no windows to the rear of the whole of the property either upstairs or down, apart from one in the shippon. There is a door to the immediate left that leads to the smaller back kitchen in which there is a slopstone under the window, a hearth against the shippon wall and the stairway on the back wall. Robin remembers hearing the cows kicking against the dividing wall while in the back kitchen. The original washing boiler was in the far corner opposite the stairs.

The only door to the shippon was at the rear and there was a second window at the front. In the stable one enters through double doors under an archway; to the left is a toilet and washing boiler. The original privy is outside, attached to the rear of the stable wall, and a five-barred gate is located between the rear of the shippon and the rear of the Elephant and Castle. The front garden consists of a vegetable patch and flower borders on each side of an earth path approach to the front door. There is a row of fruit trees to the left and an outside log and wood store at the side of the stable. It is not known when the building was mostly demolished but the part that was the shippon still stands.

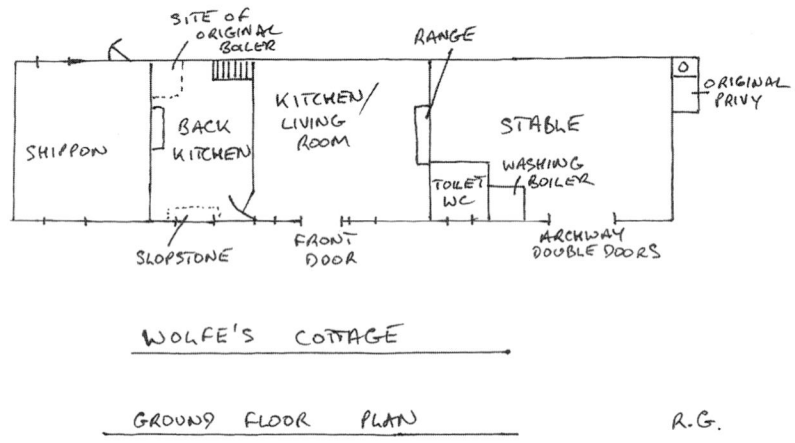

A ground floor plan of Wolfe's Cottage.

Wolfe's Cottage, The Elephant and Castle, Shavington. Robin was born here and his great grandmother, Mrs Ray, sits outside the front door.

Section 2

SOUTH-EAST

Lost Buildings around Nantwich

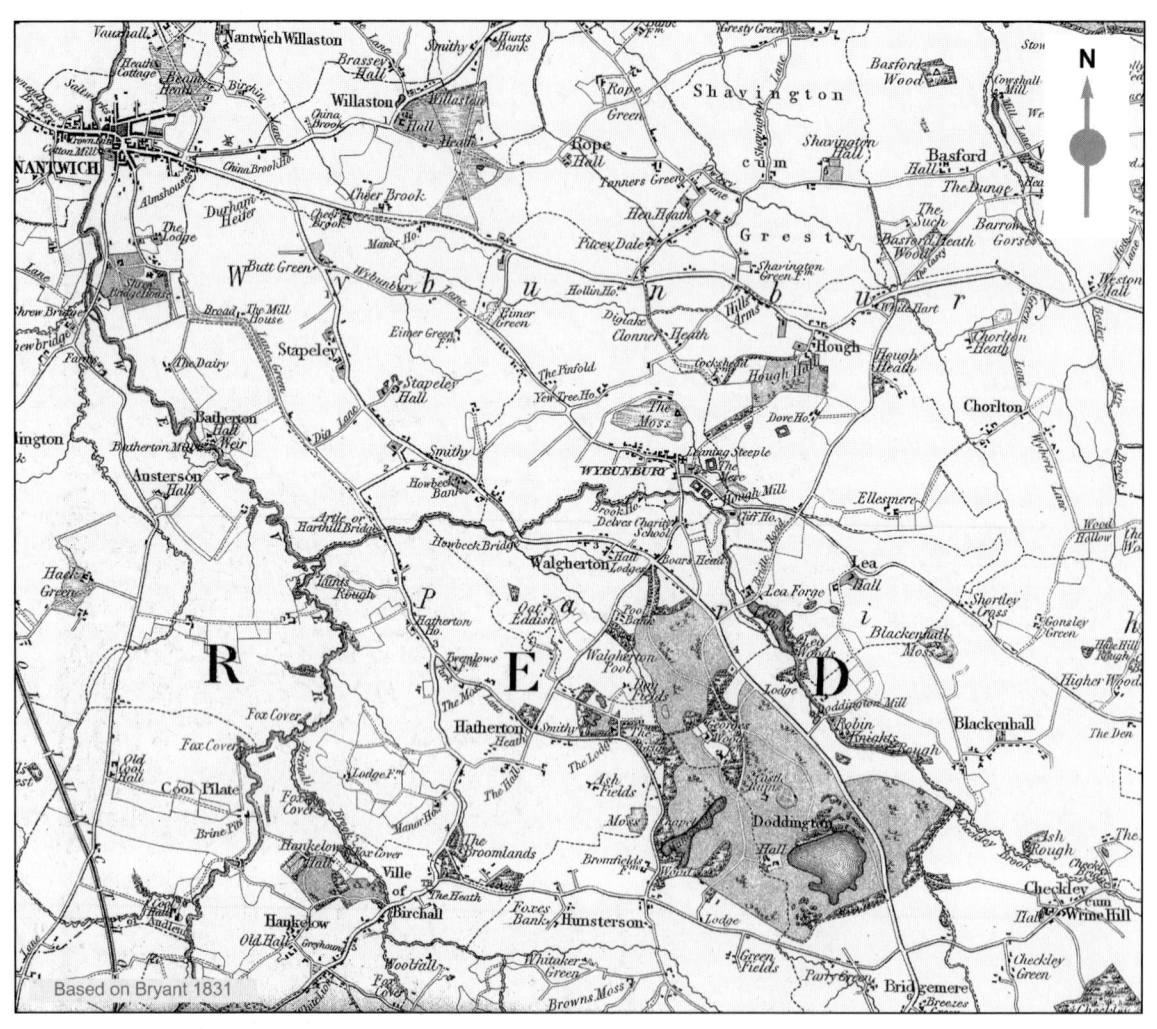

STAPELEY

Raven's Oak, London Road

This building stood in London Road on the left-hand side when going to Woore, after Foolpenny Hall and where a new housing estate stands. Charles Rainford Edleston lived here in 1874. Latham records that Edwin Reginald Bellyse, JP lived here in 1892, Thomas William Lovatt in 1910, and Lt Col Richard Banastre Crosse, a veteran of the First World War, in 1939. The buildings were demolished around 2000 to make way for the new housing referred to above.

Raven's Oak, London Road, Stapeley, demolished c.2000.

Cottage, Howbeck

There was a cottage that stood in the fields in the triangular piece of land between Newman's Lane, Second Dig Lane and London Road at Howbeck. There is no trace of it now.

Stapeley Farm, Audlem Road

Stapeley Farm still stands at the time of writing but is thought to be due for demolition in the near future. It stands on Audlem Road just after the newly created junction with traffic lights to Stapeley. It was previously in the occupation of the Johnson family.

Stapeley Farm. This building still stands in a derelict condition. It was last lived in by the Johnson family.

Stapeley Farm showing the barn at the rear.

South-East

The barn at Stapeley Farm.

The Horse and Jockey, Audlem Road

At 125, Audlem Road can be found the house which at one time was a beerhouse called The Horse and Jockey. The only item remaining from the licensed premises is the signboard which is still, after all these years, in quite good condition. The licensee was Arthur Passey. A few years later it passed to Robert Owen whose name is on the signboard. Curiously, the name of the public house is not shown on the sign. It is not known when it ceased to be a public house, but the house is still in the same family and was a shop until the 1960s.

125, Audlem Road. This building was once a beerhouse called The Horse and Jockey. It later became a shop and is now a private house.

Mrs Owen and her son Harold holding the Horse and Jockey beerhouse sign from 125, Audlem Road.

The Horse and Jockey signboard.

The Brine Baths Laundry, Audlem Road

Almost directly opposite the house previously mentioned stood the building that was once the laundry for the Brine Baths Hotel. Derek Hughes, in *The Brine Baths Hotel Nantwich*, published in 1994, has this to say:

"It is interesting to note that the Hotel had no laundry facilities of its own. All the laundry was loaded onto a handcart and taken to the Hand Laundry which was adjacent to what is now 152, Audlem Road. This Laundry is believed to have been started in the late nineteenth century by a man who came to Nantwich from East Anglia. The cottages adjacent were built originally for the laundry workers. A Nantwich Guide, dated 1913, states that the owner at that time was a man named George Chapman. The actual building which housed the Laundry and resembled a large garage was demolished in late 1994."

The Brine Baths Laundry, Audlem Road, demolished in 1994.

The Tollhouse, Audlem Road

This building is still standing but is thought to have been extended from the original. It still retains the two front windows typical of tollhouses when they were used to watch for oncoming vehicles from both directions. It was originally built by the Nantwich to Market Drayton Turnpike Trust and ceased to function as a tollhouse when the Turnpike Trusts were wound up in 1875.

The Tollhouse in Audlem Road for the Nantwich to Market Drayton Turnpike Trust. It stands on the corner of Batherton Lane.

The same building from the opposite direction.

194 and 196, Audlem Road

There were two wooden bungalows side by side here and owned by the same family. No. 196 was demolished some time ago and replaced by a modern house. No. 194 was demolished early in 2006 and is to be replaced with a two-storey building.

This picture shows the wooden bungalow at 194, Audlem Road in the process of demolition.

Stapeley Mill

Two fields to the north-east of Maylands Farm are marked on the 1838 Tithe Map as Near and Far Mill Fields to the west of what is now a bridleway known locally as Deadman's Lane. This reference suggests that a mill stood here many years ago and it is most likely to have been a water mill. Dodgson contains a reference to a mill at Stapeley in 1347. The Tithe Map shows the lane with access from London Road. It stops about three-quarters of the way down and this could indicate where the site of the mill was. There are no remains visible now. Also, Maylands Farm is called The Mill House on the 1831 Bryant Map. On later maps this name changed to Mile House and a more recent adaptation has turned it into Maylands.

The Smithy, 64 Broad Lane

This building was standing until about 2001 when it was virtually demolished and a new house was built on the same site.

Old House in Broad Lane

An old black and white house stood in the field nearly opposite 112 and 114, Broad Lane. This is undoubtedly the one described by Mercer as follows:

"House built of timber in the late 17th century. It is of one storey and an attic of two cells. There is a hall, now heated with a 19th century fireplace which possibly replaces a firehood, and two small rooms, presumably a parlour and a pantry. The door was on one long wall into the hall; the stairs could not have been in their present position by the stack if there was a firehood but their original position is uncertain."

Grove Farm, Audlem Road

This was one of several smallholdings that were built along Audlem Road by the County Council in 1911. Gwen Goldstraw's family moved here in the mid-1930s. Although not actually demolished it has undergone a recent reconstruction.

Grove Farm, Audlem Road, Stapeley. This building, built in 1911, has undergone a major reconstruction.

Artlebrook Farm

This farmhouse is still standing but has been given a brick surround so that its appearance belies its early timbered origins. However, the offset front door does give some clue. The building is thought to have been built in the seventeenth century, possibly with ship's timbers said to be reclaimed from the Dee estuary near Chester, and contains internal chamfered beams. It belonged for many years to the Delves Broughton family in whose possession it was in 1838. The occupier then was Thomas Birchall. The Goldstraw family have lived here since the 1950s.

Artlebrook Farm. This seventeenth-century farmhouse still stands but has been encased entirely with brick, belying its early origins.

BATHERTON

Batherton Mill

Dodgson contains a reference to Batherton Mill in 1351, and it is known that the manor of Batherton including the mill originally belonged to the Barons of Nantwich, from whom it passed to the Audleys. It was sold in the reign of King John to Bertram de Griffin of Baddington. In the middle of the seventeenth century, Richard Griffin and Jane, his wife, sold the manor to Thomas Delves and it was passed down through succeeding generations of the Delves Broughton family.

In 1850, the miller was John Whittingham (he was also listed as being at Hough Mill in 1834). As John Whittingham junior is listed here in 1860, and 1874, he might be the son of the John Whittingham at Hough Mill.

The Norris report in 1964 refers to the remains of the mill where a footpath now crosses the river, beneath which are three arches. There is a three-foot high wall still standing on one side. He suggests that there may have been two small wheels at each end of the mill or one large wheel in the centre of 12–13 feet diameter and 4 feet wide, and probably undershot. The single central wheel is considered most likely as the remains of the wheel can sometimes still be seen at low water in the river bed just downstream of the central arch. According to Derek Brookshaw, who was born there and whose father, John, was the last miller and also a wholesale butcher, the building was a three-storey building that was tall and narrow. It was demolished around 1925. His grandfather, William and great grandfather, also William, were millers here, the last named being listed at Crewe Mill at the bottom of Mill Street in 1860.

Early maps show the only access road to be from the Austerson side of the river. There are no remains of the sluice further upstream at what was known as the Fender Hole. The original river bed can just be traced in the fields now, the present river course having been cut originally to form the mill race.

Roy Cope, whose family lived for many years next door at Batherton Hall, remembers local children swimming in the river here around the 1930s.

The remains of Batherton Mill. The mill wheel was originally under the central arch.

This is known as the Fender Hole at Batherton Mill. The sluice gate was used to divert water away from the man-made mill race on the right The original path of the river to the left has since been filled in and there is now no sign of sluice gate or sandstone blocks seen in the photograph.

WYBUNBURY

Blakelow Chapel

Hall mentions a reference in Bishop Gastrell's *Notitia Cestriensis* to a meeting house for Anabaptists with about 40 members. The meeting house stood in a field called Chapel Field, almost on the corner of Haymoor Green Road and Newcastle Road. There is also another field called Chapel Field adjacent but in Stapeley parish. There was previously a cottage on the site which may have been the building in question. Hall also mentions that Thomas Pedley, aged 75, remembers old people telling him in his youth that stones from the graveyard were used up in building cottages in the neighbourhood, and the Wybunbury Parish Registers contain an entry as follows:

"1723 June 1st Elizabeth Dunbibb, a stranger, interred at Blakelow Meeting House within the Township of Wibunbury."

In *Wybunbury*, edited by Frank Latham in 2003, there is a reference to houses registered for religious purposes which says:

"1692 a certain house newly erected in Blakelow."

This would undoubtedly be the building mentioned above. In the same book there is mention of a small font found in 1959 at Blakelow, thought to have been used by an early nonconformist community, and this would tie in nicely with the information above.

In 1846, the cottage was owned by Mary, Eliza and Emma Hill and the occupier may have been William Mainwaring.

A building called Sunberrie House now stands on the site of this cottage. Rather confusingly, there is thought to be a Quaker burial ground at the Drift House, a black and white building which is some 500 yards away, nearer to Shavington but on the same side of Newcastle Road.

Yew Tree Farm, Annions Lane

The original farmhouse was a small black and white cottage with a thatched roof. It had an extension to the rear with a catslide roof and a larger two-storey later extension on the north side at the rear. Photographs taken immediately prior to demolition in the mid-1980s show a bulge in the side wall.

Left: A seventeenth-century farmhouse at Yew Tree Farm, Annions Lane prior to demolition.

Above: Another view of the same farmhouse from the side.

Daisy Hill, Far Waygo

On the Tithe Map of 1846, the site is described as two houses, garden and road (that would be Waygo Lane). The owner was Joseph Tew (farmer at Howbeck Farm) and the occupiers were Widow Jervis and another.

In 1881, it appears as a single property, now called Daisy Hill. Thomas Shenton, agricultural labourer aged 29, was living here in the fields after the end of Waygo Lane, with his wife, two sons and two daughters. The building was still standing in *c.*1910 but some time later was demolished. All that remains now are a few bricks lying on the ground in a small triangular copse.

Moss Lane

In 1846 there were five cottages in Moss Lane. In 1881, the five cottages were still there. Now there are just three properties: Shone's Dairy at Moss Farm; the building opposite called The Moss; and further down the Lane, Moss Nook Early maps show at least one cottage to the west of Moss Farm.

The Black Horse Inn, Main Road

This building is still standing and its address is No. 30, Main Road, on the corner of Kiln Lane. The licensees were as follows: 1841 and 1851, John Green; 1861, Elizabeth Green; 1871, William Brereton; 1881, James Newton; 1892, Sarah Newton; 1895, Thomas Symcox; 1914, Samuel Lowndes. It appears to have closed shortly after this. It is now a private house.

No. 30, Main Road, Wybunbury. This was at one time The Black Horse Inn.

St. Chad's Church

Although the fifteenth-century Wybunbury Church tower is still standing, the main body of the church has had several rebuildings due to subsidence beneath. It is recorded that an early building was replaced in 1591 and the chancel demolished and rebuilt in 1641. The next major rebuild was in 1760 and there is an illustration of this church presented to the parishioners by local landowner and historian John Twemlow, Esq. Sadly this building also suffered subsidence problem and the chancel had to be completely rebuilt in 1791.

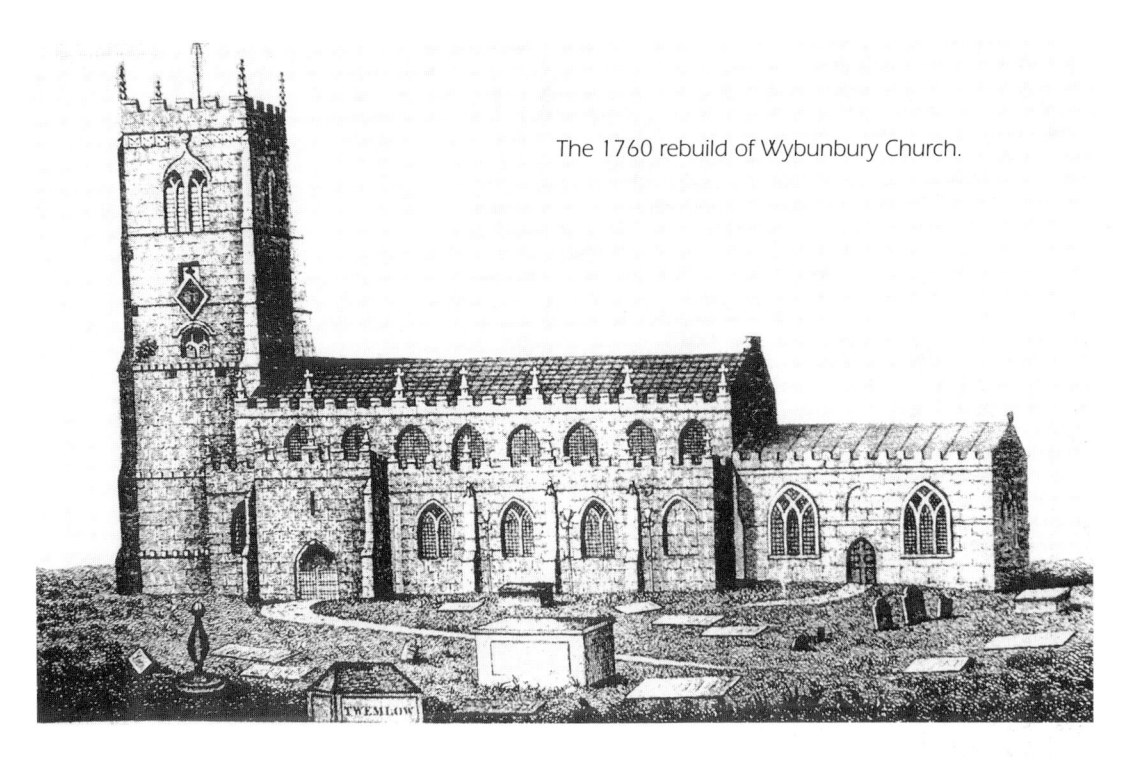

The 1760 rebuild of Wybunbury Church.

Another view of the 1760 rebuild. The hearse house can be seen to the left of the tower.

Another view of the church looking east, entitled 'The Hanging Steeple of Wybunbury', which must have been drawn around this time, shows the hearse house to the north of the tower. It is recorded in the Churchwarden's Accounts that the hearse house was replaced by a new building in 1795. After further subsidence problems, the well-known engineer and architect James Trubshaw was called in to straighten the tower, which he duly did in 1832. He also demolished the old church and replaced it with a new building some thirty feet to the south of the previous church. An illustration of the Trubshaw church dated 1836, also presented by John Twemlow, Esq, shows the rather plain exterior and it came under much criticism from the architect's contemporaries. A gap between the nave and the tower can be seen but the northern aisle was attached to the north-east corner of the tower.

The Trubshaw church, however, suffered the same fate as its predecessors and a decision was taken to rebuild in 1891. The architect of the new church was James Brooke and he built the church with the intention of copying the 1760 design. It did not quite materialise like that due the extensive underpinning required absorbing most of the cost. Further ground movement in more recent times has proved fatal to this rebuild and it was demolished in 1977. A new church was built on a completely different site in Main Road. The tower was successfully underpinned and now stands alone on this site.

The Wybunbury Tower Preservation Trust is a registered charity and its trustees are proud of the fact that they were consulted by representatives from the world-famous leaning tower of Pisa and were able to suggest a method of straightening, first used successfully with water by James Trubshaw in 1832.

An illustration of the Trubshaw-designed Wybunbury Church with the Free School, dated 1836.

St Chads Wybunbury at the turn of the nineteenth century showing the 1891 and final rebuild. The church was demolished in 1977 but the tower survives.

St. Chads Wybunbury, interior of the 1891 rebuild.

The Free School, St Chad's churchyard

In Latham, there is a reference to the Free School in the Churchwarden's Accounts in 1687, when the cost of mending the schoolhouse, daubing and making a window cost 2s. The school was thought to have been attached to the church and must have been made of wattle and daub from the reference. It was taken down and replaced by a new building funded by public subscription in 1760 and it can be seen as a separate building to the north of the Trubshaw church in the illustration of 1836 mentioned above.

In 1852, the Free School in the churchyard was taken down and some of the materials from the building were used for the new school in Main Road to the west of the church. A plaque on the front of the building, now used as a village hall, records this.

The Hospital of The Holy Cross and St George

The c.1875 OS 1st Edition map shows the ground to the south of the church to be called Hospital Bank. In Latham there is a reference to this mediaeval hospital that was founded before 1464 and dissolved in the sixteenth century. It may have been similar to the two hospitals or hospices in nearby Nantwich also existing at this time.

Wybunbury Mill

The 1838 Tithe Map shows two fields near Wybunbury brook more or less between the little estate called Churchfields and the brook. They are called Mill Field and Mill Meadow. There is no trace of a mill here now but the names of those two fields give a strong indication that there was a mediaeval water mill here at one time. Dodgson has a single reference, to a millfield in 1549. Although not far from Hough mill, it was in a different manor or parish and so it could be a logical site. Apparently, it was of a similar age to Hough Mill and the buildings were raided by villagers for house building in the fifteenth century. There would have been a track to the mill at one time and so the existing footpath over the brook could help to locate this site.

Brook House Farm at the end of Sally Clarke's Lane, Wybunbury.

Brookhouse Farm, Sally Clarke's Lane

The old farmhouse is still standing at the time of writing and a modern house has been built very close to the old building. It stands not far from the Mill Meadow mentioned above and one may wonder if there may have been some connection to the mill at some time. The Tithe Map of 1842 shows that it was in the ownership of Sir John Delves Broughton and occupied by Thomas Vickers. The house has been in the possession of the Cooper family for some time. It is expected that demolition will occur in the near future.

Houses, Bridge Street

Three new houses at nos 20, 20a and 22, Bridge Street, just to the north of Sally Clarke's Lane, mark the site of two old cottages which stood here. Apparently Bridge Street was called Grubb Street in the *c.*1910 OS 3rd Edition map. Also a bungalow opposite, at 31, Bridge Street has replaced an older cottage that once stood here.

Hough Mill

Norris records that this was only a small mill, by then (1964) largely demolished, with only some stonework of the weir and foundations of the mill being visible. Stonework can still be seen on both banks of the brook but there does not appear to be any sign left of a weir. The site of the manorial mill was created as far back as 1241 by the Bishop of Lichfield. According to George Riley in *Ancient Water Wheels on Checkley Brook*, published in 1987, the mill did not appear to be profitable by 1814:

"It was advertised – To be sold by auction – assignees of Abraham Rosson, bankrupt of Nantwich – 19 February – powerful water corn mill, situate at Hough – 4 pairs of stones."

John Whittingham is listed as the miller in 1834 and in 1848 it was Joseph Dutton. In 1850 it was Dutton and Pickford and in 1860, again Joseph Dutton. It is still shown as a corn mill in 1875 but by *c.*1910 it had closed.

WALGHERTON

Howbeck Watermill

The Tithe Map of 1842 shows the large field to the Hatherton side of Howbeck brook next to Howbeck Bridge to be called The Mill Hills. This suggests that there was a watermill here at some time. There were also two cottages here that may or may not have been associated with the mill. They were owned by Sir John Delves Broughton and occupied by William Latham in that year and described as two dwellings and a garden.

Walgherton Windmill

On London Road, Walgherton, as one proceeds towards Woore after the Boar's Head, the second house on the left-hand side of the road is called Mill House. It stands quite near the top of the rise and would have been the miller's house. From the lie of the land it could only be a windmill here. This is confirmed as a windmill and is shown on a Delves Broughton Map of 1815. It is, however, not shown on either an earlier map of 1762 or a later one of 1842.

Inn, London Road, Walgherton

Opposite Mill House stands a building that is at one time thought to have been an inn. This building has now been divided into two dwellings. On the south side, the house used to be called Old Timbers but has recently been renamed Whitebriar Cottage. On the north side is Ivy Cottage.

Hillcrest, London Road

As one continues towards Woore, just before the junction with Back Lane is a small bungalow called Hillcrest which at the time of writing is due for demolition. It has been sold with planning permission for a replacement building on that site. It would appear that the bungalow is not very old, perhaps built in the 1950s to 1960s.

Hillcrest, Walgherton. This is due for imminent demolition at the time of writing.

Dagfields

The Walgherton Tithe Map of 1842 shows the original Dagfields situated to the north-east of the present farm. Its access was from Lodge Lane. In that same year, it was owned by Sir John Delves Broughton and occupied by Peter Moor and described as house, buildings, orchard and stackyard. The buildings were still there c.1875 but had disappeared by c.1910 with the present Dagfields Farm being shown instead.

The original buildings can be clearly seen on the enclosed Bryant Map of 1831.

Windmill, Dagfields

A Delves Broughton Map of 1762 shows a windmill field just to the north of the old Dagfields and therefore points to the site of a windmill at an earlier date.

Hussey's Nook, Sandy Lane

The 1842 Tithe Map shows two cottages here. One was owned by Mary Sparrow, tenanted by George Brown and described as cottage and garden. The other was owned by William Jervis, tenanted by Martha Latham and described as dwelling house. One of these cottages was in a ruinous condition for many years and was demolished in 2006. In this tiny cottage lived Mr and Mrs Shervel. Mr Shervel was a little man and he wore a special shoe as one leg was shorter than the other. Mrs Shervel was a big lady and wore a sack around her waist as an apron. There was a row of painted blue stones in front of the cottage which were cleaned every week.

In the other tiny cottage, now derelict, lived Mr and Mrs Speed and their three children. It still stands, and is a two-celled house with an attic of two bedrooms. The front door is at the end of the house and one enters into the kitchen/living room. There is a black kitchen range against the central chimney stack. To the side of this is a doorway into the front room or parlour in which there is a fireplace at an angle against the chimney stack. On the other side of the range in the kitchen/living room is a door leading to a back pantry and adjacent stairs to the upper floor. The only windows in the upper floor are one in each gable end. Ceilings are low and there are chamfered stopped beams on the ground floor. Both ground-floor rooms had only one window each, so it must have been rather dark inside. After the family left it was used by the Dakin family from Oat Eddish to store potatoes.

Left: Cottage at Hussey's Nook, Walgherton. This was originally thatched and the photograph shows the front and side.

Above: The same cottage showing the rear and side walls.

Left: Another view of of the cottage at Hussey's Nook.

LEA

Lea Forge

There are references to Lea Forge in an article entitled 'The Charcoal Ironmasters of Cheshire and Lancashire 1600–1785' by B. Awty taken from *The Transactions of the Historical Society of Lancashire and Cheshire* Vol. 109 dated 1957. Apparently both Lea and Doddington Forges were established around 1650 by Sir Thomas Delves to produce coldshort iron for the nail industry. This iron, made from local ores, had proved to be more suitable for nails than the softer iron ores previously produced in Furness and the Forest of Dean. There is, unfortunately, no further information regarding Lea Forge apart from a reference to a Mr Hopkins who held the lease here in 1783. It appears to have closed soon after, but Awty does say that:

"Lea Forge was the last survivor of the charcoal ironworks of Cheshire, not being dismantled until 1890, though this was long after any connection with the charcoal iron industry had ended."

The Tithe Map of 1838 shows a row of seven cottages near the pool, but unfortunately it is impossible to locate the exact site of the forge. On the same map, Hammer Meadow is shown to the north-west of the cottages mentioned.

Lea Forge Mill. The mill wheel is said to have come from the mill at the end of Mill Street, Crewe.

Lea Forge Mill

It is not clear when Lea Forge Flour Mill began operations and whether it occupied the same building as the forge. It is shown clearly on the *c.*1875 1st Edition OS map. The miller in 1851 may have been John Brookshaw, aged 39 and listed as agricultural labourer. Also listed is James Brookshaw, aged 50, miller's servant. There is a reference in Riley, from a directory of 1892 that refers to the Forge Mill occupant as Edward Charles, farmer and miller. It was still shown as a corn mill in *c.*1910. Norris reported on a site visit in 1963 that the building was occupied by North Western Farmers and was in good condition. There was an iron wheel outside, under a canopy, which was said to have been transferred from Crewe Mill at the bottom of Mill Street. The wheel appeared to be of breast type and very wide. The tail race had been filled in. The building has since been demolished and all that remains is the extensive millpond, a rather nice little waterfall on the side of the millpond and a penstock used for opening the sluice.

Lea Forge Farm

The farmhouse and outbuildings are still standing at the time of writing (2006) but appear to have been derelict for some time. Its future is uncertain. In 1851, John Godwin, aged 36, farmer of 156 acres and employing four labourers, was living here.

Lea Forge Farm. This is still standing in 2006 but is in a derelict condition.

BLAKENHALL

Farm, Mill Lane

The *c*.1875 OS map shows quite a large farm and buildings opposite what is now called Rosemary Cottage. It was demolished before *c*.1910 as there is no sign of it on the OS map of that year.

CHECKLEY

Checkley Mill

Oliver Bott wrote an article called 'Cornmill Sites in Cheshire 1066-1850. Part 6: Mills Recorded 1701–1850' in *Cheshire History* Spring 1986, and refers to a watermill north of Checkley Hall that was on Checkley Brook or its tributary, shown on the Burdett Map of 1777. This is the only reference to a mill here. On visiting the site, a few remains of sandstone can be seen in a field, confirming its position on the tributary to Checkley Brook.

House at Checkley Green

The Tithe Map of 1842 shows a house at Checkley Green to the right of the lane as one proceeds down Checkley Green Lane towards Checkley Green Farm. The occupier that year was John Silvester and it was owned by the Delves Broughtons family. It was still standing in *c*.1875 but had gone by *c*.1910.

DODDINGTON

Doddington Inn

A Delves Broughton Map of 1815 clearly shows Doddington Inn just to the south of the original entrance gates to Doddington Hall. There is no record of a licensee here around that date.

The enclosed Bryant Map of 1831 shows the original entrance to the Hall at right angles to the main road and situated almost opposite the Leygrounds. There was a completely different approach to the Hall than the present one as the driveway ran parallel to the main road, past the lake and joined up with what is now the main entrance and in those days was called Wilbraham's Walk. Some time later the entrance was changed and the present lodges, called Lake and Avenue Lodge, were built, with the approach to the Hall being only along Wilbraham's Walk.

Middle Lodge

As one travels towards Nantwich, at the next entrance to the Doddington Estate, on the left-hand side as one enters the Estate, stood a lodge called Middle Lodge. It was built after 1811, can be clearly seen on early maps and is simply marked on the enclosed 1831 Bryant Map as Lodge. It was demolished some time after *c*.1910.

Doddington Camp in 1945 showing some of the many buildings there. There were over 100 but none remain now.

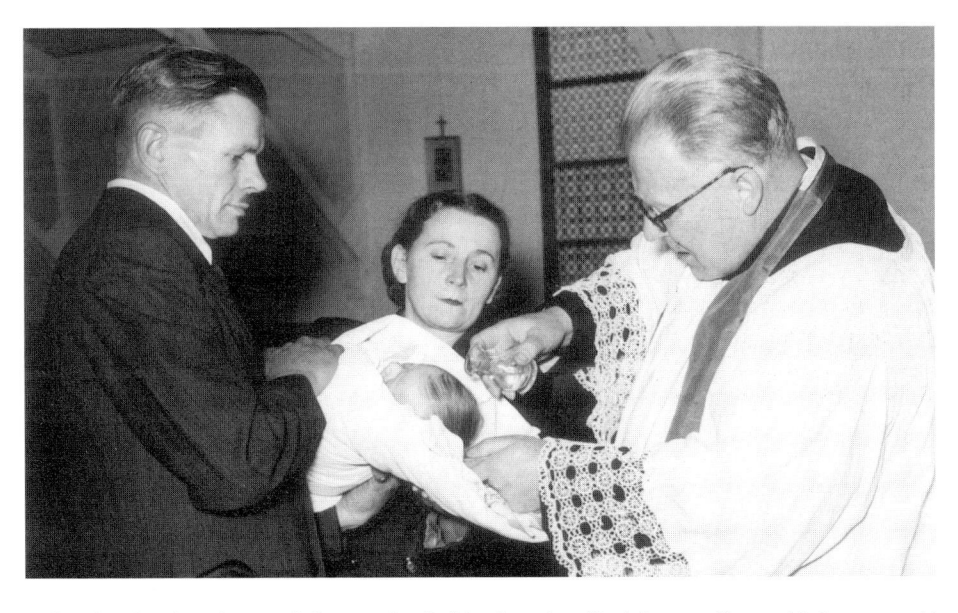

A Polish priest baptises an infant at the Polish chapel at Doddington Camp. Mr Laganowski was the godfather of the baby.

On the right is Mr Laganowski who was in charge of the Polish camp at Doddington from 1946 to 1960. His wife Gwen is in the middle with a friend on the left.

Polish inmates at Doddington Camp. Some of the buildings can be seen in the background.

Doddington Camp

During the Second World War, part of the Doddington Estate was used by the War Office and a large camp was used by British, American and Belgian troops followed by Free French sailors and finally, immediately after the war, by Polish refugees. Latham records that the camp was situated north of Doddington Hall around the church and the old castle monument, started in July 1946 when the US Army moved out, and closed in July 1960.

"It was administered by Mr Laganowski, who had been a captain in the Polish army. As well as the 109 barracks and four isolation blocks there were a variety of other buildings, including dance hall, shop, kindergarten, cinema, social club, first aid post, fire brigade, wash house with shower blocks, and school buildings. Most of the children attended the Polish School on the site. But many also attended Wybunbury Delves School and the admission records for 1949 to 1952 show 13 children from the Polish Camp. There were generally two families to each barrack, so when full there could have been 200 families or upwards of 1,000 people. When closed in 1960 there were still 12 families left, who were rehoused by the Council."

Doddington Forge

The earlier mention of Lea Forge contains a reference to Doddington Forge. This was established at the same time as Lea Forge. and we know that Doddington Forge was used for the casting of forge hammers and anvils. Awty records that:

"Though a coldshort hammer or anvil did not last many weeks, it did have the steely quality necessary for the heavy work it had to carry out, and hammers and anvils of good quality were transported for many miles."

Riley has more information to add:

"In December 1667, Sir Thomas Delves's agent agreed to supply thirty five tons of the Coltshire Iron pig metal at £4 14s per ton long weight and five tons of hammers and anvils to Cranage forge. In 1717 its output of tough pig iron was 500 tons. In 1766 the furnace was using 1100 tons of haematite ore to keep it in full blast during the year and much of this was carried from Frodsham in carts across Delamere Forest. However in 1781 the land tax assessment for Doddington shows no mention of the furnace and it would appear to have been disposed of. By 1892 it was a corn mill and a local directory gave the occupant as Joseph Edwards (exors. of) farmer and miller, Doddington Mill.

"The mill received its water along the leat nearly a mile long, connecting with a weir built on bricks and still partly visible on the Checkley Brook."

It is not certain where the forge stood but it was probably in the old Doddington Mill building.

BRIDGEMERE

Bridge Cottage

An interesting half-timbered cottage stood probably where the present Bridge Cottage is now, near the ford in Dingle Lane in Bridgemere. In Mercer, it deserved a mention as being a good example of local vernacular building. It is described as late seventeenth century, of single storey with an attic and a single storey lean-to on the west wall. It is suggested that the stairs were to the west of the chimney and the room to the south may originally have been open to the roof. It is not known when the building was demolished, but it was probably in the early 1970s.

Bridge Cottage, Bridgemere. A small timber and brick cottage no longer standing. (Crown Copyright NMR)

Seven Stars, London Road

Seven Stars cottage stands on the roadside on the left just before reaching Bridgemere Nurseries when journeying towards Woore from Nantwich. The name of the cottage is enough to indicate its probable use as a licensed premises and therefore probably an alehouse, although there is no mention of it in MacGregor, or in any directories.

Farthings Farm

This building was thought to have been a public house at one time. It is now incorporated into the offices of Bridgemere Nurseries.

HUNSTERSON

Badger's Bank Farm, Hatherton Road

Badger's Bank Farm lies derelict on Hatherton Road, Hunsterson. It was until 2005 in the occupation of the Mitchell family but its future is uncertain.

Badger's Bank Farm. This is still standing in 2006 but in a derelict condition.

School House, Hunsterson

The Tithe Map of 1842 shows the school house with the occupier Ann Martin who presumably was the schoolmistress. Its position would appear to be at Woodside opposite Manor Farm. It is not certain if it is the same building as the present one.

HATHERTON

Birchall Brook Mill

Both Hunsterson and Hatherton Tithe maps show mill fields next to each other on Birchall Brook. There is a footpath which crosses the brook and it is thought that this may well be the site of the old mill.

Birchall Moss Tollhouse, Audlem Road

The tollhouse is still standing at present but there are significant alterations being made to the building at the rear at the time of writing. This small building stands as a reminder of the days when major roads were turnpiked and travellers had to pay a toll on passing through. It stands against the roadside and has windows so that the road can be seen in both directions. The tollhouse keeper in 1842 was Joseph Deakes. It ceased to be a tollhouse around 1875.

The Tollhouse, Audlem Road, Birchall Moss. The window at the side can be seen for sighting approaching traffic.

The Tollhouse from the opposite direction.

Cottage, Oakes Corner

The Hatherton Tithe Map of 1842 shows a cottage on Oakes Corner just to the north of the present four houses. It is described as a homestead and garden and was owned by Sir John Delves Broughton and occupied by Sarah Cope. It is shown as possibly two cottages on later maps. It is not known when it or they were demolished.

Black Brook Mill

Two fields called mill fields on the Tithe Map point to the presence of a mediaeval water mill on Black Brook. These fields are situated just behind what is now a small wood part way along the entrance driveway to Lodge Farm, Hatherton, near Oakes Corner. Apparently the brook is called Black Brook and rises near The Broomlands, crossing the main road near Hatherton Manor and eventually flowing into the River Weaver.

Holly Farm, Crewe Road

This building is thought at one time to have been a public house.

Cottage, Audlem Road

The Hatherton Tithe Map of 1842 shows a cottage set back from the Audlem road just to the south of the Park Lane junction and on the other side of the road. It was owned by Sir James Delves Broughton and occupied by James Stretch. It had gone by c.1875.

The Lodge, Hatherton

On a map of Hatherton surveyed by Thomas Fenna in 1827 and drawn by Isaac Perry of Walgherton in 1828, there is a clear drawing of The Lodge. As this map was presented by John Twemlow to the townsmen of Hatherton and shows various coats of arms of the Twemlow family around the edge, it is assumed that John Twemlow lived at this house. The only building fitting the layout and marked John Twemlow is one situated a few hundred yards west of the current Hatherton Lodge and would have been somewhere behind what is now Highfields on Crewe Road. It faced north-east towards Wybunbury. The drawing shows a substantial residence with two wings on each side of the main building together with a two-storey porch of similar design. Both wings have bay windows with crenellated tops as has the porch. The upstairs windows appear almost floor to ceiling in size and contain many small panes. The front doorway is of gothic design above which are two coats of arms of the Twemlow family. It is known that John Twemlow was a keen historian. There are no traces of this building now.

Cottage, Park Lane

The Hatherton Tithe Map of 1842 shows a cottage in the field opposite Hatherton Farm Cottage. It was in the ownership of John Acton and tenanted by George Reay. There is no trace of the building today.

1 and 2 Willow Cottages, Park Lane

These two cottages were combined into one dwelling but demolished around 2002. It was the home of Mr Maddocks. A new house now stands on this site.

Chapel Farm, Audlem Road

The old farmhouse here was black and white and similar to Artlebrook Farm. When it came to demolition, the front wall needed very little help to fall, suggesting that perhaps there were no foundations. The house replacing it was built in two stages.

Artlebrook Smithy, Audlem Road

The Hatherton Tithe Map of 1842 shows a house and outbuildings just to the south of Artlebrook on the west side. It was owned then by the Tollemache family, tenanted by Joseph Prince and described as Latham's Lease. The buildings were still there in 1872 and a smithy is shown in the fields behind but had gone by *c.*1910.

Artlebrook Paper Mill

The Hatherton Tithe Map of 1842 shows a field called Paper Mill Field and Meadow on the south bank of Artlebrook not far from Artlebrook Bridge. There are still remains of this mill in the brook and on one of its banks. Surprisingly there is no reference to this mill on an earlier map of Hatherton dated 1828. It does, however, show Artlebrook Bridge as having three arches. This could well be correct as the present bridge has a keystone dated 1848 which obviously replaced the earlier one. There are no other references to a paper mill here.

HANKELOW

Hankelow School

In *Audlem*, edited by Frank Latham in 1997, there is a reference to Hankelow C. of E. School (1870–1977):

"The school was housed in a brick building built in 1870 near the Green and village pond. In 1876 a chancel and sanctuary were added. The building was licensed and became a church where regular Sunday services were held until it was demolished in 1977 and a development of bungalows built on the site. In 1902 the pupils were 66 in number. The headmistress was Miss Paget whose pay was £70 per year plus a free house, furniture and coal. The assistant teacher was Miss Lythgoe. Her pay was £35 per year. The pupil teacher Miss Woolrich received £12.10s per year."

Hankelow School. There was a pulpit inside used for Sunday services. The building was demolished in 1977.

Section 3

SOUTH-WEST

Lost Buildings around Nantwich

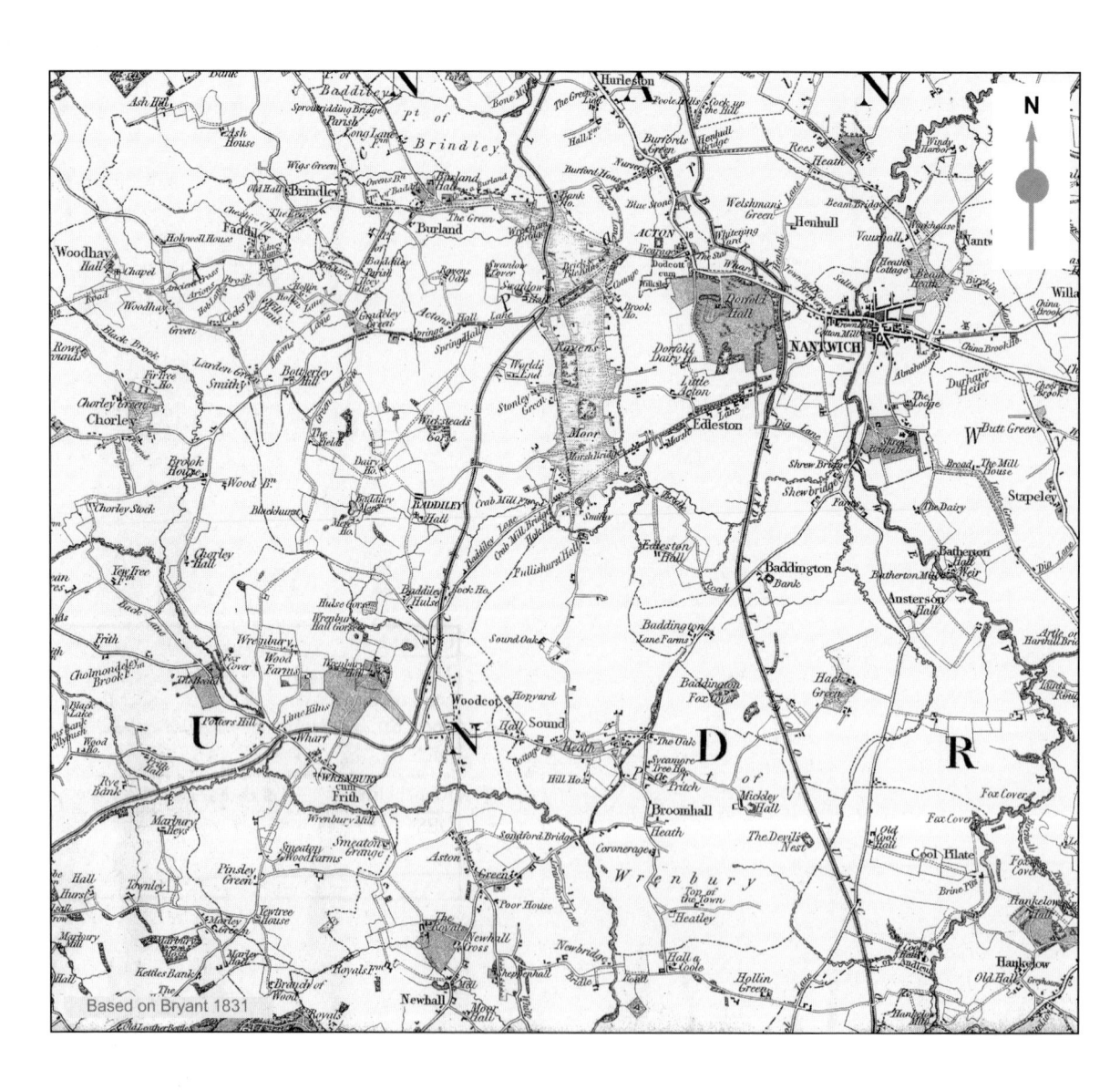

Based on Bryant 1831

AUSTERSON

Austerson Old Hall

Although this building is not lost in the real sense, it is lost to the immediate area and has had some alterations made to it. It is, however, considered important enough to be given attention.

Mercer includes this building as a good example of local vernacular architecture. He describes it as:

"House built of timber in the early to mid 17th century. It has two storeys and an attic and is L-shaped on plan with the hall and service rooms in the main range and a short parlour wing across the N. end. The entrance is into a lobby against a stack which appears only to have heated the hall originally ... The parlour wing projects to the W. and is jettied to W. and E. A large amount of panelling remains on the ground and first floors ... The walls of the parlour are in close studding with a middle rail and straight tension-braces; the ground-floor walls of the main range are bricked, but on the first floor the panels between the studs are wider and approximate more closely to small framing."

In the early 1970s, a local architect, James Brotherhood, saw the house in poor condition and decided to buy it, dismantle it and move it to a new site at Alvanley, around 20 miles away on the edge of Delamere Forest. It had stood empty since 1968 when the tenant had moved to the new farmhouse close by. An article in the May 1974 issue of *Deesider* gives a full account of the move and reports that:

Austerson Old Hall in its original position prior to removal in 1974. (Crown Copyright NMR)

"Instead of being the dominant feature of the immediate landscape, the hall had been pushed into the background by an entirely new house."

The house was duly bought, official permission obtained, all relevant timbers numbered, dismantled and re-erected on its new site. It was originally thatched judging by the pitch of the roof. Relatively modern small-paned windows were replaced with mullioned windows more in keeping with its mediaeval origin and other fixtures and fittings obtained to give the house a more authentic feel. The result is a truly remarkable achievement and shows what is possible with old buildings.

Austerson Old Hall in its new setting at Alvanley, near Frodsham. Apart from a new dormer window and the removal of the Victorian porch it is little changed from the previous picture.

RAF Hack Green

In 1941, RAF Hack Green was established as a radar station providing radar cover between Birmingham and Liverpool, on a site previously used as a bombing decoy site for the railway centre at Crewe. Several small buildings were erected during the war, one of which was an operations block known as a 'Happidrome' in a compound 250m to the north-east of the original building opposite Hack Green Cottages. This was thought to have been operational by 1943. A plan of the building shows it split into two halves, a technical side to the south-west and a domestic side to the north-east. There is no trace of the building now. Following the Second World War, Hack Green became a heavily protected 'Rotor' radar station designed to detect incoming Soviet bombers. It had a compliment of 18 officers, 26 NCOs and 224 corporals and aircraftsmen. In early1953, a domestic site was developed a mile or so south

South-West

Sgt Barker's car outside the 'Happidrome' in 1951 The two blast walls and the entrance door can be seen. The corner of Hack Green Cottages confirms the site of this early building.

4236208 Cpl Colin Bennett (Taff) outside the guardroom at the lower site, RAF Hack Green, 1962.

Lost Buildings around Nantwich

RAF Hack Green domestic and technical site c1960

1 Airmen's married quarters
2 Officers' married quarters
3 CO's residence
4 Station sick quarters
5 WRAF rest room
6 Guard room, armoury and cells
7 Fire tender building and gym
8 Store
9 Officers' mess
10 Air Ministry Works Directorate (AMWD) office
11 Bulk fuel compound
12 Stores
13 Education block
14 Station HQ
15 Sergeants' mess
16 Motor transport garage
17 NAAFI including shop, bar; lounge and airmen's mess
18 Ration stores
19 Airmen's single quarters
20 NAAFI accommodation
21 Car park (site of former airmen's mess)
22 Boiler house
23 High level water tank

68

Flt Lt Hamilton at his desk, lower site, RAF Hack Green in the early 1960s.

Doris Donnelly, Phil Ostle and Carrie Hassall at the lower site, RAF Hack Green 1963/4.

Lost Buildings around Nantwich

The members of Billet 46b, lower site, RAF Hack Green in the early 1960s.

The building that is now the Secret Nuclear Bunker at the upper site, and, to the right, the guardroom which has since been demolished.

of the radar station. By October of that year, the camp numbered around 35 structures, being a mixture of temporary Nissen type huts and a smaller number of brick buildings. At the end of the decade, the number of buildings had increased to around 60.

The enclosed map shows the layout of the domestic site. The brick houses still survive but all the other buildings were demolished in the early 1970s.

In 1958, Hack Green became an important joint civil and military air traffic control centre. It closed as an RAF Station in September1966. In 1976, the upper site was purchased by the Home Office and converted to a protected regional government headquarters at an estimated cost of £32 million. The building is partly above and partly below ground. It became operational in 1984 and remained in readiness until 1993. It is now a museum with many items of interest from the Cold War period.

COOLE PILATE

Brine Pits Farm

This farmhouse is named after the brine pits which were sunk nearby at the edge of the river Weaver some time in the seventeenth century. The search for brine proved unproductive. A later tenant here was Thomas Furber, who kept an interestingly detailed diary of his Cheshire cheese production and sale, some time around the end of the eighteenth century. In 1828, its tenant was Thomas Leech. He was still there in 1851 when he was aged 53. In 1861, the tenant was Thomas Furber, aged 36, and he was still there in 1881. He must have died some time later because his wife Mary is listed as principal householder in 1991.Their son Edwin took over the farm after this date as he is listed as principal householder in 1901.

The farmhouse was demolished in 1953 and a modern building now stands on the site.

Rear view of Brine Pits Farm, Coole Pilate. The frontage faced the River Weaver close by. This building was demolished in 1953 and replaced with a modern structure.

Coole Pilate Halt

In *By Great Western to Crewe* written by Bob Yate and published in 2005, there are some photographs of the railway halt on the now dismantled Nantwich to Market Drayton railway. They show the timber platform and waiting shelter on the downside of the track. According to Derek Hughes, in an article entitled 'A Forgotten Railway' in a *Crewe and Shrewsbury Passengers' Association Newsletter*, it was opened by GWR in 1935.

"The Halt was built by one Railway Joiner assisted by local labour. It was constructed entirely of wood, including the platforms and had a passenger shelter on both the Up and Down platforms. It was unstaffed and passengers obtained tickets from the Guard on the train. It was lit by paraffin lamps which were serviced at Nantwich and Audlem stations and taken out and back daily on the first and last trains. Passengers alighting there had to be seated in the carriageway nearest to the Guard. The Halt was used mainly by fishermen coming out of Crewe and Nantwich to fish in the adjacent canal. There was a public footpath level crossing over the lines at the Halt. It was also used by local schoolchildren attending secondary schools in Nantwich and especially Market Drayton on a Wednesday for Market day. It was not used much by service personnel at RAF Hack Green as it was too far on the Audlem side of the camp."

In the same article there is a report of a fatal accident at the Hack Green crossing (much nearer Nantwich on French Lane) on one foggy morning in 1943, when an express goods train collided with a motor vehicle carrying a party of 17 airmen and Waafs, resulting in two deaths and fourteen injured in the RAF party.

In Yate there are also other photographs of the 1950s BR signal box and the rather ornate crossing gates before dismantling in 1970 at the Hack Green crossing.

Coole Pilate Halt on the Nantwich to Market Drayton railway line. This photo was taken in 1935, shortly after construction. From left to right are Renie Bebb (who lived at Brickfield House adjacent to the Halt), Freda Bebbington and Winnie Williams.

South-West

BADDINGTON

The Raven Inn

The only evidence that a beerhouse of this name stood here in Baddington is an entry in the 1861 Census that reads 'Thomas Duckers aged 64, beerseller'. It is difficult to locate its exact position but it was only two houses away from Baddington Bank Farm in the Census return.

EDLESTON

Edleston Mill, Shrewbridge

There are early references to Edleston Mill: in the Cholmondeley family papers the mill and fishpond of Edleston is mentioned in 1297/8 and Ormerod refers to:

"The inclusion in the manor in 1348 of a lane from Edleston to the rivulet (this would be Edleston Brook) of a mill at Shrewbridge."

In 1655, the miller is named as Randle Davenport. The mill site can be identified from the position of Mill Field in a map of 1676 and is near to the site of Newbold.

Cottage in Marsh Lane

A cottage stood in the field in Marsh Lane between Manor Farm Cottages and Moss Cottage. It was of brick with wood timbering, a central chimney and thatched roof. It was in a ruinous condition for many years and was demolished around 1990.

The remains of a cottage in Marsh Lane near to Moss Cottage.

Another view of Moss Cottage.

Hawke's Cottage, Marsh Lane

This building has quite an interesting history. It is thought to have been divided into two parts of one third and two thirds. The right-hand third was thought to have been an alehouse called The Raven and there are stories (unsubstantiated) that it was frequented by Dick Turpin. The entrance door is on the side of the cottage and the stairway faces it. It is known that William Boote lived here in 1786 and the widow of Samuel Jones in 1838. There is a beerhouse keeper called John Haywood listed in Edleston in 1850 but it is not certain if he lived here. The building was dismantled in the late 1970s with a view to it being re-erected at Tatton Park. This never materialised and so the pieces remain on a local farm awaiting re-erection at some time in the future.

Hawke's Cottage, Edleston. Part of this building is thought to have been a public house.

South-West

SOUND

Amson's Cottage, Whitchurch Road

On the Sound Tithe Map of 1841, there is a cottage shown to the east of the entrance driveway to Hill Farm. It was called Amson's Cottage. It was still there in 1872 but was demolished some time after this.

The Red Lion, Sound Common

The name of Red Lion Farm suggests that at one time this was a licensed premises. The owner in 1841 was Henry Taylor and the tenant James Hollins. There are two beerhouse keepers listed under Sound in 1850, namely John Boote and William Whittingham, and whether there is any connection with the above premises is unknown. The farm is currently an abattoir.

Malt Kiln, Sound Hall

This building is currently (2006) still standing and is in use as a barn but is shortly to be converted into a private dwelling. Malthouses or malt kilns were common some 200 years ago but there are practically none still standing intact and so this is quite an interesting building. There is a long section of the building with two storeys and a low ceiling to the ground floor which is paved with quarry tiles. This is where the malt and hops were dried.

The malt kiln, Sound Hall, showing the drying area for malt and hops. There were two floors and six wooden shutters to each floor to adjust air flow through the building.

The same building showing the end section where the ale was brewed.

There are six windows with wooden shutters hinged from above, on each side, to control air circulation through the drying floors. The taller part of the building on the end and at right angles to the drying floors was used for brewing, but oddly there is no evidence of a chimney. This part was also later used as a stable. The hop yards in the fields behind Sound Hall are clearly shown on the enclosed Bryant Map of 1831.

The malt house may well have supplied the local ale and beerhouses mentioned elsewhere in this book and it is thought that one of Sound Hall Cottages was an alehouse at one time.

Sound Hall Cottage

It is thought that there was a cottage to the west of the present Sound Hall Cottages near the railway line. It is not known when it was demolished.

Appletree Fields Farm

This building stood to the west and slightly north of Sound Oak. In 1841 the farm was described as house, yard and garden. It was owner-occupied by Thomas Dickenson. It was still there in *c.*1910 but was demolished some time later.

RAVENSMOOR

The Barracks, Barracks Lane

The name of the lane suggests that there was a barracks here at one time. No other evidence to support this claim has so far been found.

The Smallpox Hospital, Hospital Lane

There is a very interesting article in the January 1950 issue of the *Nantwich Chronicle* regarding the smallpox hospital, titled 'Forgotten Hospital has had patients, but the last one was 35 years ago!'

"For over 20 years Mr James Langley, aged 69, former butcher, has assiduously looked after his tiny eight-bed smallpox hospital at Ravensmoor, near Nantwich, but not a doctor, or nurse, or patient has he seen there in all that time! In fact, he has given up hope of ever doing so.

"Each day, Mr Langley, assisted by his wife, lights the stove in the hospital and the fires in the adjoining nurses' bungalow to keep the place aired and ready for use. The floors are kept spotlessly clean, the windows polished and the paraffin lamp wicks neatly trimmed; but the peaceful atmosphere of this little hospital, tucked away from view in the green fields of the countryside, has remained undisturbed by any event so strange and rare as the arrival of an ambulance with a smallpox victim!

"For all these years, Mr Langley, who lives nearby in 'Hospital Cottage', has maintained the hospital in a spick-and-span condition, sharing his duties of caretaker with those of keeping a cow, rearing poultry and cultivating his garden.

"He has put fencing round the hospital, repaired the gates etc. and actually diverted a sewer which ran under his cottage. And every day he wondered whether the next day would bring him his first patient. But Mr Langley is now more concerned about his own future than patients, for the hospital is to be sold by its new owners – the Manchester Regional Hospital Board – and he does not know what will happen to him. He has heard no word from the authorities.

"The story put out last week, however, that Ravensmoor's smallpox hospital has never had a patient since it was opened some fifty years ago is incorrect, for the records show that the hospital has had nine cases (one fatal) and one suspected case. Even so, one has to go back 35 years to trace the last occasion on which the place was used. A Crewe woman was at that time admitted to the hospital where she died.

"Formed in 1901, the Joint Hospital Board acquired three cottages and some land in Ravensmoor in 1906 from a Mrs Ann Roberts, Norbury, but it is evident that the hospital existed before that date and it is likely that it was built following an outbreak at the end of the 19th century.

"Mr H.G. Atkinson, formerly Clerk of the Nantwich Rural Council for many years, recalls that the hospital was built by a contractor named George Ginger and he thinks that it was put up in a hurry in order to be ready for any further cases. In December 1902, the hospital probably had its first case – a patient from Hospital Street, Nantwich – and the following year there were seven patients there. Another one was admitted in 1904, and the last recorded case was the fatal one referred to – in 1915. Subsequently, a casual was admitted from the old Nantwich Workhouse as a suspect, but the case was not confirmed.

"Mr A.E. Whittingham, Clerk of the former Joint Hospital Board, says that so far as he is aware there was never any resident staff at the hospital, assistance being obtained from other local hospitals when required. The hospital, added Mr Whittingham, was kept in good condition in spite of its empty beds and was available for use in 1948 when the Joint Hospital Board ceased to function and the hospital passed over to the State. Near to the hospital stand the three cottages which were bought nearly 50 years ago. Two are derelict, and the other is the house of Mr Langley who took over the job of caretaker from his brother-in-law Mr Tom Davenport, Larden Green, leaving a butchering business which had been in his family for over 100 years to do so.

"Parallel with the hospital is the nurses' bungalow, made of asbestos and wood, on a brick foundation and a more attractive structure than the hospital itself. It has a marked 'sunshine'

Ravensmoor Smallpox Hospital. It was taken down in the 1960s.

atmosphere, with its many and spacious windows and glass doors and in addition to domestic facilities, it has a bathroom, two bedrooms and a verandah which overlooks a picturesque dingle. The hospital is of corrugated iron on a brick foundation with a wooden internal lining. There are two wards and eight beds (now minus the bedlinen), a doctor's room and a bathroom. Neither building has electricity and the only form of lighting is by paraffin lamp."

The Folly, Swanley Lane

A house of this name stood on the site of what is now called St. Andrews Court. It was apparently a two-up two-down cottage and was a smallholding belonging to Bert and Amy Eley. It is thought to have been demolished around the 1980s.

NEWHALL

Kingswood Green Methodist Chapel

In Latham, *Wrenbury and Marbury*, there is a reference to this chapel: "this was a tin structure built by George Cliffe on his Kingswood Green Farm. George was a member of the Plymouth Brethren. It was demolished early in the twentieth century."

Whitmore Hall Cottage, Sheppenhall Lane

The present, modern Whitmore Hall stands just behind where a small cottage stood at one time. It is not known when this cottage was demolished.

Sheppenhall Hall

The hall is thought to have been built in 1671 and plastered in the eighteenth century. It had ornamental woodwork, oak beams and panelling. It was significantly repaired in 1850. It was owned by the Court family for 250 years and farmed by the Youngs between 1843 and 1921. Richard Massie was living there in 1850 and in 1860 it was Mrs Mary Massie. It was finally demolished in 1958 but the outbuildings have been converted into separate dwellings. Parts of the old moat remain.

Sheppenhall Hall, demolished in the 1950s.

Newhall Castle

Close to Sheppenhall Hall stood Newhall Castle. James Hall argues that this was not a castle as such but more likely a fortified manor house. It was originally the seat of the Audley family, which descended to the Foulhursts, and then finally the Crewe family. It is not known when it was demolished.

Newhall Windmill

The Newhall Tithe Map of 1842 shows two fields called Windmill Bank and Mill Pool, and Windmill Field. These are both just to the west of the watermill site and show the previous presence of a windmill. The fields were owned by Viscount Combermere and the occupier was William Brereton. It is not unusual for a windmill to be superseded by a watermill on a nearby site and the same can be seen at Hankelow.

Newhall Watermill

There are various early references to Newhall Mill and it is not known if they refer to the windmill or watermill. In 1645, Thomas Cartwright of Cholmondeston, Gent., became the tenant of Newhall Mills and in 1683 William Bullock became the miller.

On one of the original walls of the mill is an inscription dated 1790 that says the mill was reconstructed by one Hazeldine of Bridgnorth, a prominent ironwright of his time who provided the great Telford with castings for the Menai Suspension Bridge in North Wales. There was a large millpool here and other back-up pools upstream, one on a field on Smeaton Wood Farm known as Adamley Pool. The pool can be seen on the enclosed Bryant Map of 1831. This millpool was later filled in and the road realigned so that the mill was no longer on the roadside.

The Mill was later converted to steam, and in 1842 William Brereton was the miller at the watermill and steam mill. The miller here in 1850, 1860 and 1874 was John Pearson. Latham refers to the last miller here (maybe John's son):

"William (Billy) Pearson would, when he had finished work for the day, listen for a while at the mill door to make sure all the machinery had ceased to function."

The mill closed early in the last century.

Newhall Dairies

The Creamery was started by a group of local farmers just prior to the First World War who got together to run a cheese factory, and was called Newhall Farmers Dairies. In *Wrenbury and Marbury*, edited by Frank Latham in 1999, there is a reference as follows:

"There is a report in the *Whitchurch Herald* dated 5th June 1913 headed 'Cheese Factory opened at Newhall – local farmers enterprise.' The old corn mill was converted into a cheese factory, operated by steam power, and when in full production could deal with 1,800 gallons of milk per day, turning out 17cwt of cheese from three 500 gallon vats ... Initially six men were employed."

In 1930, when it became a subsidiary of the Cheshire Sterilised Milk Company of Stockport, its name was changed to Newhall Dairies Ltd. It was refurbished in the 1950s to become a model creamery, and taken over in 1954 by United Dairies, but still under the control of the Keeling family from Stockport. It later became a Unigate factory named Aston Creamery when United Dairies merged later with Cow and Gate, and then became a Dairy Crest Creamery when sold in 1979. During the mid-1960s it was handling 45,000 gallons of milk daily during the peak season in early summer, turning it into some 15 tons of cheese and 10 tons of whey powder. The quality of its Cheshire cheese around this time was exceptional, with over 75% of its production graded as Extra Selected, the highest grade attainable, and many prestigious awards were won at various shows including the London Dairy Show.

It was Dairy Crest Aston's bad luck that it was chosen as the only site in the country for the ill-fated large-scale production of Dairy Crest's new Lymeswold soft blue cheese. All the old cheesemaking plant was replaced with a modern continuous machine made of stainless steel in 1983 and geared to produce around 4,000 tons a year with 24-hour production. It was hoped to compete against the French Brie and Camembert soft cheeses but despite a loyal following of over one million customers, it never achieved anything like its full potential and production was finally stopped 10 years later in 1992 and the Dairy Crest Factory closed. It was later sold to Gordon Plant at nearby Moor Hall Farm who has since let it to New Primebake from Telford who now use the premises as a bakery.

Exterior view of Newhall Dairies in the 1930s.

One of the cheese stores at Newhall Dairies in the 1930s.

Exterior view of Newhall Dairies in the 1950s.

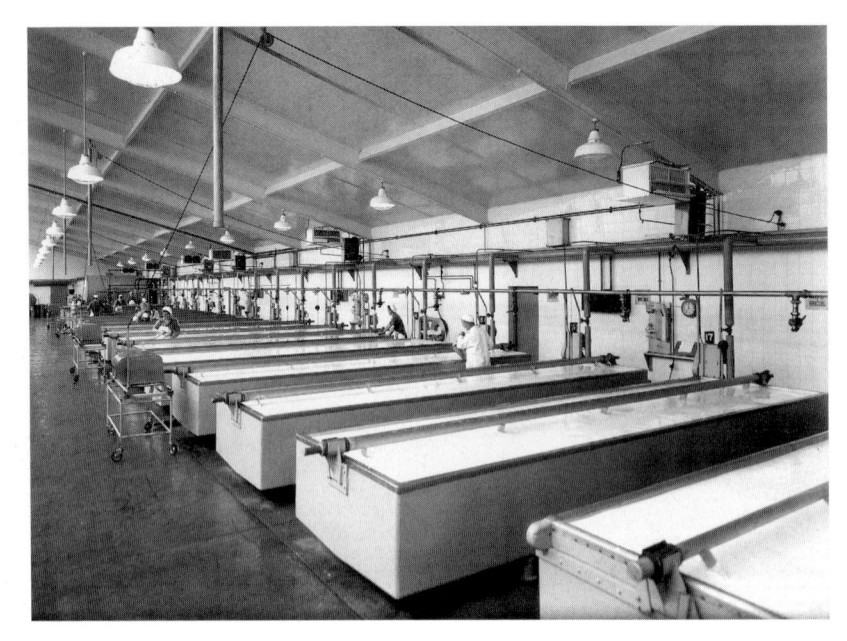

Newhall Dairies vat room in the early 1960s. The man in the white coat is Tom Seaton, Production Manager.

Tom Long (on left) and Bill Welch, breaking the Cheshire curd by hand in the traditional way at Newhall Dairies in the 1950s.

South-West

Cheese in store at Newhall Dairies in the 1950s.

The press room at Newhall Dairies in the 1930s with some cheeses removed from press and bound in cloths.

Newhall Dairies in the 1950s: roller drying of whey to produce whey crumb which was then ground to a fine powder with a hammer mill. This was quite an unusual method of drying whey.

Part of the mechanised stainless steel continuous cheesemaking line used for making Lymes-wold cheese at Dairy Crest Aston in the 1980s. This was on the same site as Newhall Dairies.

Welch's Smithy, Newhall

This building was located just off the main Whitchurch Road and modern offices belonging to New Primebake Bakery have been built here. It was still standing in 1910 but demolished some time later.

Welch's Smithy at Newhall c.1900. The offices for New Primebake now stand on this site.

Two Cottages, Whitchurch Road

There were two thatched cottages on the Whitchurch Road just to the north of the above smithy. The nearest one to the smithy was called The Nook; it only had one bedroom and Harry Jennings lived here. Next door was The Brooklands. It had two bedrooms and May (née Welch) and Phillip Griffiths lived here. Both cottages had long gardens stretching down to the brook. Part of the car park for New Primebake is now where the gardens were.

The Cheshire Cheese Inn, Whitchurch Road

This building stands back from the road near Newhall Cross. The site is marked as Newhall Cross on the enclosed Bryant Map of 1831. The house is now divided into two halves called The Rowans and Newhall Cross House. At one time it was a single building and an inn. It was licensed from 1765 to 1860 when it closed. Part of the building is also said to have been used by the Combermere Estate for its administration around these times. Later it was a Ladies' School from the 1870s to the 1890s, run by a Miss Martha Page.

Moss Side, Sheppenhall Lane

This large attractive house, built around the mid-20th century, was demolished in 2003 and three modern houses now stand on this site.

Lee's Cooperage, Aston

On the site of what used to be Stuart Graham's Garage and is now a new housing estate was a cooperage belonging to William Lee where he made wooden dairy utensils. He had a shop in Beam Street in Nantwich. He was later assisted by his son, Alfred, changing to a motor garage with Alfred's son, Rupert. There is a bungalow at the rear of the site which retains the name of The Cooperage.

Paradise Mill, Aston

This mill is marked by a footbridge which crosses the River Weaver midway between Woodcott footbridge and Sandford Bridge. There is a reference to Paradise Mill in 1686. James Hall noted in 1878 that traces of the mill dam were still visible then and apparently locals recall traces still existing in the 1930s. There are no remains now, however. There is a drawing in Latham's *Wrenbury*, which shows the old Paradise Bridge which used to span the river.

Sumner's Mill, Aston

The original building that was Sumner's Mill has been demolished. It was built around 1880 when Arthur Sumner developed the provision store and bakery owned by his father, Samuel into a corn milling and cattle feed business.

Arthur Sumner's mill at Aston. Arthur Sumner is in the foreground at the front of the left-hand cart.

South-West

WRENBURY

Wrenbury Old Mill

In Latham, *Wrenbury and Marbury*, there is a reference to Wrenbury Old Mill: "... at Mill Farm near to the railway station which some say dated back to the sixteenth century and closed at the beginning of the twentieth century. Some claim that it was called Abbotts Mill at one time. Writing in 1880, Hewitt described the site as a 'pretty place viewed from the stone bridge'. It is noted in the Sites and Monuments Record as being earlier than 1777 (Burdett), and refers to T.A. Coward's drawing in 'Picturesque Cheshire' as 'showing a large external undershot wheel with lean-to roof cover'."

This mill stood on the River Weaver. Ann Manley is listed as the corn miller for Wrenbury (most likely here) in 1850. John James Slater was the miller here in 1892. He also played for Combermere Cricket Club and there is photograph of the team of 1894 in which he is included. There are few remains of this building now and trees surround the site, making it virtually unrecognisable. The mill pool still exists. Some of the spokes from the above-mentioned millwheel are incorporated in the present house on this site.

Wrenbury Old Mill with its large external wheel. This postcard shows the mill around 1900.

Wrenbury Station

Some of the various buildings associated with the station, including booking office, waiting rooms, toilets and goods yards were either sold or taken down in 1967 after the Beeching cuts. Apparently there was even a special private waiting room built at the end of the nineteenth century, for Elizabeth, Empress of Austria, to be used when she came to stay at Combermere Abbey for the hunting season. This waiting room was demolished in 1967. There were also new sidings constructed for the railway horse boxes. Later, the sidings were used by the Trufood factory and also for coal deliveries.

Wrenbury Station looking towards Nantwich c.1905. The station opened on 2nd September 1858. The picture shows on the left a waiting room, an open area including ticket office and another waiting room.

Outbuildings at The Salamanca

The Salamanca was for a long time a public house. It is now a private house called Salamanca House. The outbuildings are thought to have been two separate stable blocks. The one behind the Salamanca was of two storeys, the upper floor of which was at one time a ballroom. It is thought that these stable blocks were taken down in the 1960s.

A gathering of the hunt outside the Salamanca Hotel around the 1920s. The outbuildings in the background have gone.

Trufood Ltd, Wrenbury Station

Again in Latham, *Wrenbury and Marbury*, there is information concerning the factory:

"In 1908, an American company built a factory, on an 11 acre site, near to the railway station at Wrenbury for the purpose of drying milk powder and eggs by a patented spray process. It thus became the largest employer of local labour in the immediate area ... In 1921 the factory was taken over by Lever Brothers who within a few years launched Humanised Trufood, its most famous baby food product. In the same year a cheese factory was built ... In the 1950s, new cereal products and 'spoonfoods' were produced for infants and a contract was entered into with the Ministry of Food to bottle orange juice. A further innovation was the production of specialised foods for infants with dietary problems. In 1955 the company was taken over by Cow and Gate and the plant was modernised ... it was a sad day for the community when, in March 1975, the Wrenbury factory closed with the manufacture of baby foods being centralised with another company. Expack Egg Processing Ltd re-opened the factory in 1976 under the managership of Tom Mason, who had previously been employed with Trufood since before the war. One million eggs were dried each week together with the manufacture of various egg products. Within a few years the factory was finally to close and since then the buildings have been used for smaller business ventures."

Above: View of Trufood factory from Wrenbury Station railway sidings taken in the early 1900s.

Left: Another view of the Trufood factory taken in the 1950s and showing the Managing Director's House on the right.

The Salamanca, Wrenbury Green

Stanley House, on Wrenbury Green, marks the site of The Salamanca, an inn, and is shown on a print of Wrenbury in 1848. Stanley House was rebuilt in 1859 when the new Salamanca was erected by the station to take advantage of the railway for the hunting fraternity. Apparently this same licensed premises was known as The Fighting Cocks from 1765 to 1828. For a short while it was known as The Lord Combermere but by 1834 it had become The Salamanca.

Thatched Cottages, Wrenbury Green

Next to Stanley House stood four thatched cottages in a row and one of the middle ones was at one time a shop. These cottages were later demolished and two semi-detached houses called 1 and 2 The Green stand on this site.

An illustration of Wrenbury Green in 1848, dedicated to Samuel Sproston, Esq. of Sproston Wood, a local benefactor. The Salamanca, the four thatched cottages and the Round House on the right have all gone. (Copyright reserved)

Thatched cottages on Wrenbury Green taken in the early 1900s. The middle cottage was a sweet/haberdashery shop run by the two Miss Lloyds, who are shown standing outside. These cottages were demolished in the 1930s and replaced by two properties.

South-West

A postcard dated 1908 showing one side of Wrenbury village green with Stanley House to the left, the four thatched cottages (on the previous illustration), the row of five cottages with the Round House at the end and Green Farm, which was also the village Post Office.

A modern aerial view of the same side of Wrenbury Green. The thatched cottages have been replaced by two white semi detached houses. The black and white farm on the right of the upper photo has also been replaced by a modern brick house.

The Round House

This small building stood at the end of the row of cottages called Nos 3 to 8, The Green. It may at one time have been a village lock-up as they were often called by that name in the nineteenth century. However, it is thought that it may also have been a girls' school. In 1850, Wrenbury Girls' School had 26 pupils. It was occupied by Arthur (tailor) Jones until around 1900 when he moved to Oak House. It is thought that the Round House was taken down around this time.

The Hearse House

This building stood for many years down a lane at the end of the Green, just beyond the above properties. It is believed to date back to 1851 when it was given to St Margaret's Church by a local squire and was used to house a glass-sided hearse for the use of the local villagers up until the early 1920s. It was once used by a local family to keep pigs in. In the early 1930s, it was used by J.T. King (the local builder) as a garage. Later the building was owned by Mrs Roe. Around 1990 it was demolished, despite some efforts being made locally to save it.

The Hearse House with Roy Blackburn, Chairman of Wrenbury Parish Council at the time the photo was taken in 1991. Roy was instrumental in a campaign to save the building which was unsuccessful.

Green Farm, Wrenbury Green

This farmhouse was originally an oak-framed, thatched black and white building of the sixteenth century and can be seen quite clearly on old photographs of Wrenbury Green. It was the home of the Vaughan family for many years. Tom Vaughan (1799–1873), who lived here, was the last dog whipper or beadle for Wrenbury Church. It became the village post office around 1890, run by his son John. After he died it was carried on by his wife, Harriet until the late 1920s when the business was transferred to John Sheen at No. 2, The Green. The black and white building was demolished in the late 1950s and replaced with a modern brick building.

Green Farm, a black and white timbered building now showing a tin roof. It was also the local Post Office.

Walter Hockenhull's Butcher's Shop, Wrenbury Green

There was a butcher's shop here to the west of Green Farm. It stood in the garden belonging to Dr Loney and later Dr Patterson, where two houses, Byways and The Vicarage, now stand. It is understood that this wooden shop was constructed in the late 1930s and was in use until the early 1960s. After standing empty for a while, it was burnt down in the mid-1960s by persons unknown.

Walter Hockenhull's butcher's shop, taken in the 1950s. In the foreground, left to right, are John Whittaker, Geoff Garnett and Frank Hayes.

Weaver Farm, Wrenbury Green

This farmhouse was one of four working farms on the Green. This list also includes Green Farm, Church Farm and Wrenbury House. It stood on the corner of the Green near to New Road and was the home of Tom Garnett, who farmed here in 1902. He was also a wheelwright, joiner and undertaker and the last Poor Rate Overseer in 1926. Oliver, his son, was also a wheelwright and joiner, served in World War One, and later took over the farm. There was a small cottage at the end of Weaver Farm in which Sam Heath, the gravedigger lived. He was succeeded by his son Tom, who was also a gravedigger and lengthsman for the County Council.

Lost Buildings around Nantwich

The white building is Weaver Farm, which has been demolished and replaced with a new house. To the left is Elm House, to the right is Yew Tree House and on the right of this is Birchwood House.

Church Farm

The Young family farmed here in the 1890s. Later, Tom Hardern farmed here in the 1920s, with his son Arthur continuing until the early 1990s when the site was redeveloped.

An aerial view showing Church Farm and barns before conversion.

Church Farm and barns before conversion in the 1990s.

A modern close-up view of Church Farm and barns.

The Free School, St Margaret's Churchyard

The Free School was built in the churchyard in 1605 and founded by Ralph Buckley. It provided free places for eight pupils for ever. The schoolmaster was required to teach a minimum of eight, but if they exceeded fifty then he had to pay 40 shillings from his annual salary of £10 to employ an usher to teach. By 1860, this school had combined with the grammar school newly built in 1843, and this amalgamation continued until the present Wrenbury School was built in 1876.

A photograph showing Wrenbury Free School in the churchyard. The schoolmaster's house on the right behind is still standing.

Beech House, Nantwich Road

This house is thought to have been extensively altered in the 1930s and its frontage is quite different from the original. The current occupier was John Butler.

An early photograph showing Beech House on the right.

A modern picture of the same view showing alterations to Beach House.

Wrenbury Grammar School

This building was erected in 1843 from public subscriptions and endowed by Viscount Combermere and Samuel Sproston. As mentioned above, it had combined with the Free School by 1860. After Wrenbury School was built in 1876, it became a Sunday School. The building still stands but has been added to and is now called St Margaret's Hall.

This building was built as Wrenbury Grammar School. It later became a Sunday School. It still stands today and is used as a village hall.

Wrenbury Hostel Site, opposite The Dusty Miller

During the Second World War there were square wooden huts built to house foreign prisoners of war, many of whom worked on local farms. Peter Bebbington recalls, as a young boy, talking to some of these who were friendly and spoke in broken English. After the War, the huts were used by mentally handicapped patients, a unit which was later run by The Lady Verdin Trust. The facilities were transferred to Nantwich around 1990, and the Wrenbury site developed for housing.

Wrenbury Mill, Wrenbury Lift Bridge

Bott records the remains of a small corn mill on the east side of the Llangollen Canal by the Wrenbury Lift Bridge. It stood on the River Weaver. This would place it near the present Dusty Miller public house.

Wrenbury Mill. Buildings belonging to the mill were on both sides of the canal but the ones on the right have now gone, to be replaced by the Dusty Miller public house and restaurant.

Wrenbury Wood Barn

According to Latham in *Wrenbury and Marbury*, this is supposed to have been built in 1680. The Rev. Matthew Henry is thought to have preached in it and also from a horseblock in the farmyard adjoining.

Wrenbury Wood Barn. The Rev. Matthew Henry is said to have preached here. (Copyright reserved)

Wrenbury Hall workshops

Around the 1950s and 1960s there were workshops built in the grounds of Wrenbury Hall. These were used by rehabilitating and mental health patients (living at Wrenbury Hall hostel) for furniture manufacture, brush making and similar construction activities from which they were paid a small wage. Those activities continued until 1986 when it was sold by Cheshire County Council. The William Gibson Hostel has been extended and is now called Wingate House. The handicraft and brush manufacture buildings are no longer used.

Wrenbury Hall showing the workshops used for rehabilitation of mentally ill patients in the foreground.

Wrenbury Heath Methodist Chapel

In Latham, *Wrenbury and Marbury*, there is a reference to this chapel. It was a small Primitive Methodist Chapel at Wrenbury Heath and was demolished between the two World Wars.

BADDILEY

Baddiley Windmill

On the Baddiley Tithe Map of 1839 is marked Windmill Field, confirming the existence in former times of a windmill here. The field is to the north of Baddiley Hulse and the roadway (now called Baddiley Hall Lane) terminated here at that time. Access to Baddiley Church and Baddiley Hall from Nantwich was from Ravensmoor via Baddiley Corner and then across the fields via what is now just a public footpath.

Blackhurst Farm

The same Tithe Map of Baddiley shows an earlier Blackhurst Farm in a different location to the present one. This was obviously demolished and a newer premises built nearby some time later.

Baddiley Church

There are two line drawings of Baddiley Church from around 1810 at the Cheshire Record Office, which show the exposed timberwork from which it was constructed. They show a square framing construction with a lozenge pattern. There is also a wooden bell tower on the roof at the western end, and a small south porch. The exterior of the main part of the church was later encased with brick as it is now, but the chancel for some reason was not. The porch and wooden bell tower have also gone.

Baddiley Deserted Village

In a field to the east of Baddiley Hall lies the remains of an abandoned mediaeval village. There is evidence of at least nine tofts and crofts (house platforms and associated enclosures) situated each side of a small stream now culverted in the field. Agricultural practices have led to some surface disturbance but it is possible to make out the rough outlines of properties in the field concerned. It is presumed that this was the original Baddiley village and the question arises as to why it was abandoned. It is known that it was a grange belonging to Combermere Abbey and the Tithe Map shows the field as being called Great Grange Field. The grange extended beyond the canal as the fields on the opposite side were called Middle Grange Field, Far Grange Field and Grange Field Meadow. Archaeological excavations in the future might produce some answers.

ACTON

Houses in Dig Lane

The Acton Tithe Map of 1842 shows a house opposite Dig Lane Farm. Also approximately halfway between Dig Lane Farm and Dig Lane Cottage there is a house on the same side of the lane. This latter building had disappeared by *c.*1875 but the other mentioned earlier was still in existence until at least the 1950s.

Cottage in Marsh Lane

Again the Tithe Map shows a dwelling, described as cottage and garden, just to the west of Brook Farm. This had disappeared by *c.*1875.

House in Tally Ho Lane

The Tithe Map shows a building in Tally Ho Lane and a little further north than the cottage mentioned above. It was described as house, garden and orchard, was owned by Julia Tomkinson (of Dorfold Hall) and occupied by William Ridgway. It had also disappeared by *c.*1875.

Acton Grammar School

Latham gives an account of the above building in Acton churchyard:
"The school was founded on 26th May 1662. In 1662 thirteen trustees were empowered to hire a master at £20 per annum ... Immediately after the subscriptions were made, the trustees appointed James Clewlowe, who did not stay, and later that same year Paul Woods, an Oxford graduate, was appointed. For Paul Woods, and the masters who followed, the trustees laid

An early picture of St Mary's, Acton showing the grammar school on the left.

down certain rules and orders. Each morning school was to begin with readings from the Old and New Testaments, singing from the psalms and prayers. In summer time work commenced at 7am and at 8am in winter. There was a midday break from 11am to 1pm and the afternoon session continued until 5pm in summer and 3.30pm in winter. The Parish Sexton was to toll the morning bell at 6am in summer.

"As the name suggests, the Grammar School curriculum concentrated upon the teaching of grammar, and this was the case at Acton. Latin and Greek were both taught. In addition, the Trustees stipulated that the scholars should be catechised in the principles of religion for one hour or more every Thursday afternoon. Discipline was placed in the master's hands. Punishable offences were listed by the Trustees.

"Pupils' fees were paid according to a sliding scale. For a gentleman's son the fee was 2s. 6d. p.a., for a yeoman's son 12d. and for others 6d. The first recorded change in payment of fees occurred in 1847, when the fee for the first son of a parishioner was £4.4s. and £3.3s. for subsequent sons.

"In the third quarter of the nineteenth century the fortunes of the school declined. The deterioration set in under Daniel Chater who came in 1847. In 1861 the school closed for a period of three years, and re-opened as a commercial school. In 1885, with a debt totalling £39.14s.2d., the school amalgamated with Nantwich Grammar School ... The debt was paid by the governors of the newly formed grammar school, who then sold the Acton school building to the church wardens for £400. The building was subsequently demolished and the land incorporated in the burial ground."

Cottage near Cross Lanes House, Cuckoo Lane

There was a whitewashed cottage standing in what later became an orchard belonging to Cross Lanes House. The sexton, Mr Smith, lived there and was John Parker's grandfather.

Pilberry's Cottage, Cuckoo Lane

There was a small cottage on the corner of Cuckoo Lane opposite Keeper's Cottage. The Pilberry family lived there many years ago.

Simpson's Cottage, Cuckoo Lane

There was a cottage on the opposite side of the lane and about halfway between the black and white cottages now called Magpie Cottage and Cuckoo Cottage and Pear Tree Cottage. Apparently it had an earthen floor. The Simpson family lived there and John Parker remembers playing in the road with Bill Simpson as a child. You couldn't do that today with all the traffic!

Cottages, Cuckoo Lane

On the site of what is now called the Bungalow, close to the crossroads at Bluestone, stood a pair of whitewashed thatched cottages. The Blackburn family lived in the northern half and George Oakes lived in the other half. Later on, the Blackburn family left and George Oakes took over the other half of this cottage. George was Janet Gray's (née Oakes) grandfather and there is a picture of him thatching his house.

Griffiths' Cottage, Bluestone

This was at one time also a pair of whitewashed thatched cottages belonging to the Dorfold Estate. The building stood in front of what is locally known as "the glass house" at Bluestone. Photographs show the two front doors. The smaller part on the right was a shippon. The cottages were later amalgamated into one and the Griffiths family of 13 lived here. It was demolished in the early 1950s.

Cottage, Bluestone

The Acton Tithe map of 1842 shows a house to the north of the row of cottages at Bluestone and across the main road. It had gone by *c.*1875. It would have been quite close to where the Bluestone is now.

Griffiths' Cottage, Bluestone. This stood immediately in front of "The Glass House" and was originally two cottages. Later they were merged into one and the Griffiths family lived here with 12 children. The part on the right was a shippon.

Lost Buildings around Nantwich

The same thatched cottage with a lady thought to be Ethel Griffiths and baby in front. Note the pram.

Above: A photo of George Oakes in his seventies.
Right: George Oakes sitting outside his cottage at Bluestone crossroads.

104

South-West

George Oakes thatching his cottage.

Another view of George Oakes' cottage.

Bluestone Farm

It is thought that Bluestone Farm was at one time a public house. There is a cellar here and it is thought that it may have some connections with the Queen's Head in Welsh Row, Nantwich.

BURLAND

West View, Wrexham Road

A bungalow stood in front of the house now called West View. It was demolished during construction of the above-named house around 2002.

The Cock o' Burland, Wrexham Road

The enclosed Bryant Map of 1831 clearly shows The Cock o' Burland on the Wrexham Road, just to the south of the junction of Long Lane leading to Haughton and Bunbury. This was undoubtedly a public house and its licensee in 1841 was Samuel Hulse. It is described on the Tithe Map apportionment as a public house and garden owned by Ralph Hulse. The 1841 census lists the occupants as Samuel Hulse, aged 55, agricultural labourer, his wife Nancy, aged 61, and daughter Martha, aged 24, servant at home.

Castle Hill Cottage in the 1950s. This stands on the site of The Cock o'Burland. The lower windows are an unusual shape for a private house.

The OS 1st edition map of *c.*1875 shows the building in a similar position as the one on the Tithe Map, and it is also clearly marked as Cock of Burland. In Latham, *Acton*, there is a reference to Burland Castle, and as the current building on this site (although nearer the road than the one previously referred to) is called Castle Hill Cottage, the mention of Ralph Hulse would confirm its location.

"According to Hall's notes there used to be a building here known as Burland Castle which, he says, was 'a primitive kind of chalet, built by an eccentric gentleman, Mr Ralph Hulse, who died in March 1888 aged 80'. The building was 'demolished a few years before that date by an ill wind'. It used to be known as 'Skeleton Castle'."

The present building is somewhat eccentric in design, having two particularly large windows of almost chapel-like design to the ground floor on the side elevation. It is hard to say if any of this building contains parts of the older property.

Raven's Oak

The enclosed Bryant Map of 1831 clearly shows a building with outbuildings and named as Raven's Oak, situated on a lane which has now disappeared between Wrexham Road and Springe Lane. It stood behind Burland Farm and gave its name to Raven's Oak dairy which still operates from the farm. There is a very nice map of 1801 in the Cheshire Record Office showing the buildings and access road from Springe Lane with a cartouche of a raven sitting in an oak tree in colour wash. There are no traces of buildings on later maps.

CHORLEY

Cottage near Bankhouse Farm

A cottage stood here some time ago, not far from the farm and quite close to the brook. It was apparently destroyed by fire.

Chorley Water Mill

There is a single reference in Latham, *Wrenbury*, to Chorley Water Mill. In The Book of the Abbott (of Combermere) published in 1524, in the list of leases and rentals, Hugh Malbank includes the Mill at Chorley with its pool and fishery. Also in Dodgson there is another reference to the mill here in 1305. A possible site could be to the west of Chorley Hall where two footpaths converge at the brook.

Section 4

NORTH-WEST

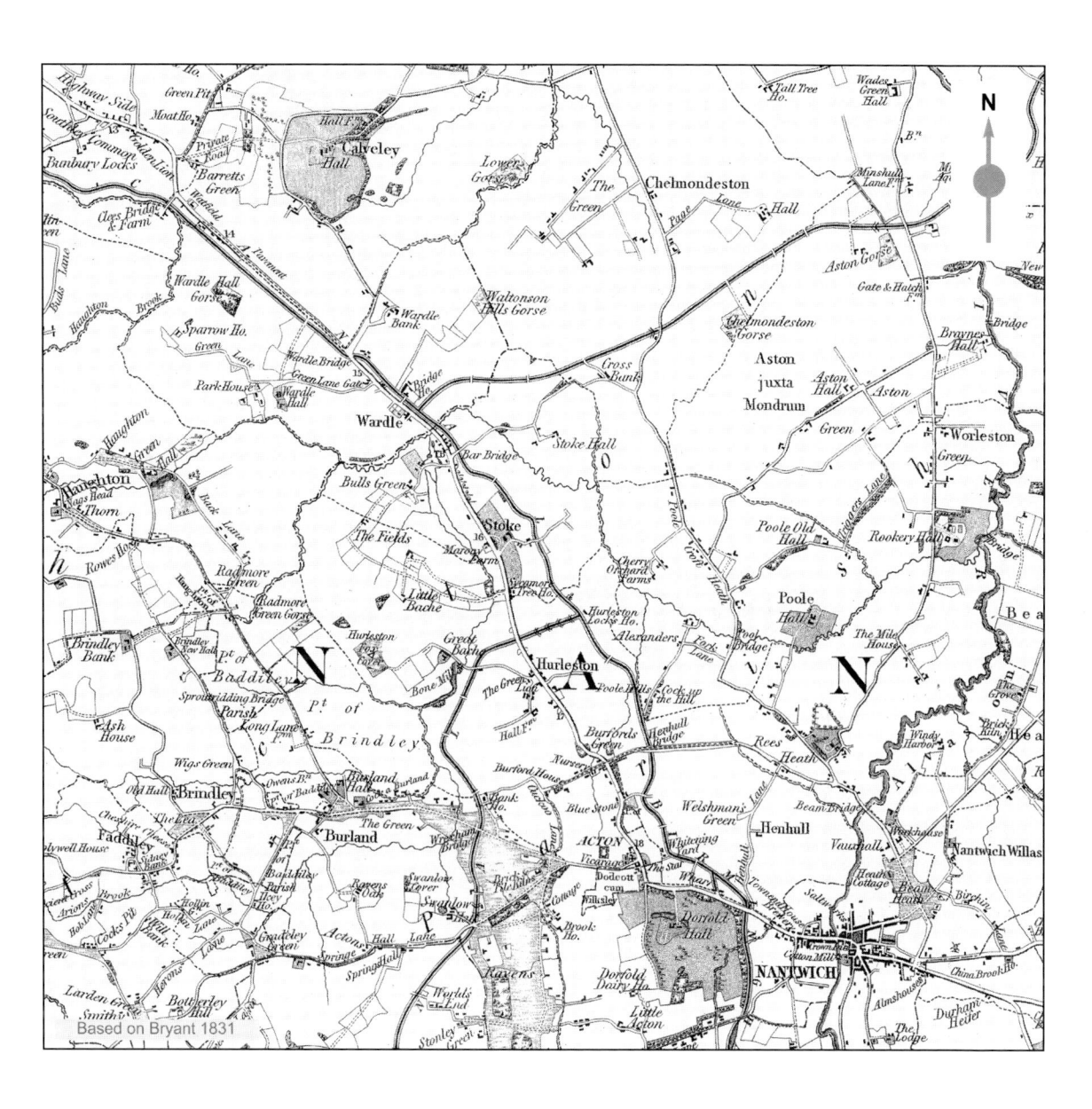

North-West

109

BRINDLEY

Thornyfields Farm

This farm stood to the west of High Ash in the fields. Its only access was from the Wrexham Road from the Ridley direction. Peter Cooke remembers the Edge family living here. It was demolished in the early 1950s.

Cottage, Capper's Bank

Lilian Parker remembers a cottage in the fields not far from Capper's Bank when going towards Spurstow. It is not known when it was demolished.

FADDILEY

Three Cottages, Wrexham Road

There were three black and white cottages in Wrexham Road opposite the Tollemache Arms (now renamed The Thatch). These were replaced firstly by a garage and a house and later the garage was replaced by two modern houses.

Woodhey Hall

In *Cheshire Country Houses* by Peter de Figueiredo and Julian Treuhertz, printed in 1988, there is a description and drawing of Woodhey Hall. This was built by Lady Wilbraham around 1690 and replaced an earlier building. It was designed by Lady Wilbraham in the classical Carolean style in brick with long and short stone quoins, tall windows, hipped roof and a parapet partly concealing the roof and typical of the period. There are dormer windows and unusual circular windows in the basement. It is not known when the hall was demolished but it is thought to have been still standing in 1857. Parts of the hall are thought to have been incorporated into the delightful Woodhey Chapel, which is still standing.

Cottage, Heron's Lane

Peter Cooke remembers Percy Woolley and his uncle living in a tiny one up, one down cottage midway along Heron's Lane (now called Hearns Lane). They slept on a straw mattress in the upstairs room that was accessed by a ladder. Apparently Percy was quite a character and is remembered by several local people. He put brown shoe polish on his legs to resemble socks and black shoe polish on his head. He would sit on the front of the stage at Acton Village Hall when rehearsals were taking place for local events. He was late one morning for work (he did the milking at Blackhurst Farm). His boss, Mr Proudlove asked where he had been. It eventually transpired that his uncle had died in the middle of the night and Percy had just rolled over and gone back to sleep. He said, "He never hurt me when he was alive and so he wasn't going to hurt me when he was dead!"

REASEHEATH

Cottages, Beambridge

The cluster of estate cottages now known as the Green, Reaseheath used to be known as the hamlet of Beambridge, named after the nearby sandstone bridge that spanned the river Weaver. The OS 1st Edition map of $c.1875$ shows several cottages here which no longer exist. The author remembers one whitewashed cottage where Stan Holland, the boilerman for Reaseheath and his wife and three children, Betty, Diane and David lived. This cottage was situated between The Bield and Worleston road end and was demolished around 1959. Attached to the cottage were a couple of garages which were used by the occupiers of The Bield, next door. This house was at one time where the factor for the estate lived and it is thought that the garages may have originally been a coach house and stable for him.

Nearer to Reaseheath College Drive and opposite what is now the Equestrian Centre to the College were two cottages and a village pump in front of one. One of these is thought to have been a public house called The Beambridge, whose licence ran from 1765 to 1819. The Equestrian Centre used to be known as the Experimental Farm at one time and that replaced an earlier building shown on the OS 1st Edition map of $c.1875$. Further cottages are shown on this map where Nos 1, 2, 3, 4 and 5, The Green are situated now. Opposite these and nearer still to the drive to Reaseheath College stood two further cottages.

Holly Cottage, Henhull. This stood close to Holly Farm at Henhull crossroads. From left to right are Jack Oakes, George Oakes jnr, Mary Oakes, Olive Oakes in front, and Joe Oakes. Mary Oakes was the wife of George Oakes, who later lived at Bluestone crossroads.

Wooden Bungalow, Worleston Road

Immediately after The Nooklands and Sunnyhurst on Worleston Road as one travels towards Worleston from Nantwich, there stood a wooden bungalow set back from the road in which Mary and Arthur Green lived in the 1950s. It is thought that Arthur was involved with the Northern Breeding Station poultry site immediately behind the bungalow. It was later was the home of John Haighton and his wife for approximately 30 years. It was demolished in the early 1980s.

Holly Cottage, Henhull Crossroads

As one proceeds towards Chester from Reaseheath, just before Holly Farm on the right-hand side stood a black and white cottage called Holly Cottage. It was here that George Oakes and his family lived before moving to Bluestone Crossroads. It is thought that the Shenton family lived here later. It is not known when the cottage was demolished.

WORLESTON

Cottages near Mile House Farm

Janet Spibey remembers two brick cottages in a derelict condition on the left of the lane leading from Main Road to Mile House Farm. It is not known when they were demolished.

Farmhouse at Rookery Hall

There was a farmhouse that stood at one time in the grounds of Rookery Hall beyond the service entrance to the hall. It is not known when it was demolished.

81, Main Road

A house with bow windows stood here at one time. The Everall family lived here. A modern house now stands on the site combined with No. 79, Main Road.

The Grange, Main Road

This stone building was demolished in 1930 leaving just the servants' quarters. It was apparently sold by the Behrens family to Mr Cookson, who bought the land and sold off the stonework.

The Grange, Worleston. The main stone-built building was demolished in the 1930s leaving just the outbuildings on the right.

Another view of the same building with the lake in front.

5. Chapel, Station Road

This building still stands at No. 20, Station Road but has received a modern frontage disguising its original function as a chapel.

The Chapel at 20, Station Road, Worleston is on the left of this early picture. This building now has a modern frontage which disguises its earlier function.

Worleston Station. The footbridge, sidings and buildings on the right have gone.

Worleston Green Farm

The original farmhouse here faced towards Rookery Hall. It was demolished some years ago and replaced by a modern bungalow.

HURLESTON

Tollgate house, Burford

Just to the north of Brook Cottage, Burford, stood the Burford Tollgate and its adjoining house. In 1861, John Moss, agricultural labourer, aged 41, lived here with his wife, Emma, also the same age, and she was the toll collector. It is not known when the house was demolished but it could have been around 1875 when the Turnpike Trusts were wound up and responsibilities of road upkeep transferred to the County Council.

The Red Lion, Hurleston

MacGregor records this public house in Hurleston and it is thought very likely to be The Green Lion shown on the enclosed Bryant Map of 1831. Its licensees were: in 1765, John Underwood; 1767–9, Elizabeth Underwood; 1773–5, Robert Lightfoot; 1777–1824, Matthew Whalley; and 1825–8, John Whalley. Later directories show Thomas Vickers here in 1850 and George Lawton, victualler and blacksmith, in 1860.

Village Farm, Hurleston

This farm is shown on the OS 1st Edition map of *c.*1875 on the left-hand side of the lane leading to the Bache House more or less opposite the smithy. It had gone by 1910.

The Bachehouse Mill

This mill is marked as a bone mill on the enclosed Bryant Map of 1831. This would have been used for grinding bones to produce bonemeal, which was used as fertiliser by Cheshire farmers. In 1860 it had reverted to a corn mill as Samuel Boffey is listed as corn miller and farmer at Bache House. It was still a corn mill in *c.*1910 but some time later it was demolished. There are, however, remains of a large millpool, attractive to waterfowl, and a stepped overflow weir.

The Lockhouse Cottage, Hurleston Junction

On the junction of the Llangollen Branch of the Shropshire Union Canal at Hurleston stood the lock keeper's cottage. It is shown on the enclosed Bryant Map of 1831 and marked as Hurleston Locks House. It is not known when it was demolished but this may well have been towards the end of the last century.

POOLE

The Cock o' Poole Hill

It is known that there was a public house at Poole Hills called The Cock o' Poole Hill and it is quite clearly shown (although called Cock up the Hill) on the enclosed Bryant Map of 1831. There is a reference in Dodgson to it in 1662 when it was called Cocapalle Hill. It had ceased to be a public house by 1842.

Two Cottages near Poole Bridge

The enclosed Bryant Map of 1831 shows a building on the roadside on the Wettenhall Road between Poole Hill Road (formerly Fork Lane) and Poole Bridge. This building was divided into two semi-detached cottages. In 1842, the Tithe Map apportionment shows that the late John Downes was the owner and the tenants were Samuel Read and Thomas Ikin. The cottages were still standing in *c.*1875 but had disappeared by *c.*1910.

Poole Mill, Poole Bridge

An old map of 1601 shows a watermill at Poole Bridge on the brook leading to the River Weaver. There are no signs of the mill now although there is a large piece of timber evidently from it lying across the brook on the upstream side.

Clematis Cottage, Poole

Apparently a black and white cottage of this name stood opposite the end of what is now called Dairy Lane, Poole. It was in between the house at Poole Nurseries and the renovated black and white cottage there called Badger's Point. It was apparently larger than the previously mentioned building.

Poole Old Hall

The Poole Tithe Map of 1842 describes Poole Old Hall as house, buildings, yard and gardens in the ownership of Francis Elcock Massey (of Poole Hall) and the tenancy of Ralph Whittaker. In 1850, the tenant was listed as William Goodall.

It was apparently a brick and timber building somewhat similar in appearance to Poole Bank Farm. It was later in the occupation of the Whittaker family and demolished in the1950s. A modern farmhouse was built in front of the old house.

STOKE

Methodist Chapel, Barbridge

In Latham, *Acton*, there is a reference to the destruction and replacement of this building:

"The church was built in 1843, and in 1927 under the dedicated leadership of Mr Samuel Bourne and the Rev. F. Cunningham was renovated and an adjoining schoolroom built. Then on the night of 8th October 1940 the building was bombed by enemy action. The chapel was completely destroyed and the Sunday School partially. By the autumn of 1941 the Sunday School had been repaired in order that Sunday services could be held there until such time as the chapel itself could be rebuilt. In the autumn of 1954 plans were ready for the rebuilding and on Wednesday, 20th October, the foundation stone was laid by the daughter of Mr Samuel Bourne, Mrs Gladys Johnson of Alpraham, Hall. By the spring of the following year the new chapel was complete…"

The Tollhouse, Barbridge

A tollhouse stood at Barbridge more or less opposite and slightly south of the Barbridge Inn public house, formerly The King's Arms. The tollgate was removed in 1875 when the Turnpike Trust was disbanded but it was used as a private dwelling until a short time ago.

Barbridge Mill

This corn mill stood just to the north of the above-mentioned public house. In 1850 the miller was George Hallmark and in 1860 it was William Cornes. In *c.*1875 it is shown as a flour mill. Norris records:

"Site now (1965) occupied by a bungalow. The leat is still well defined and the overflow weir survives. It is understood that the mill last worked about 1880."

Barbridge Mission

There is a reference to the Barbridge Mission Room in Latham, *Acton*:

"Technically this building was in Wardle and was therefore in Bunbury Parish, but the original lease was to Herbert Moore, Vicar of Acton, and dates from 1926. It was a canal-side building near to the Middlewich junction in Barbridge. In 1959 responsibility passed to Bunbury Parish and the Mission finally closed on 24th November 1972." Elsewhere in the same book there is mention of Stanley Sutton, Acton village blacksmith, being a Sunday School teacher here. It is known that there were regular Sunday services here in the 1950s. There is further information in an article in *Cheshire Genealogist*, Summer 1998, by John Elsworth. He mentions that, of 94 baptisms recorded here between 1908 and 1932, only three were of bargee children. Also, in 1959, the Vicar of Bunbury inherited an active Sunday School under the leadership of Stanley Sutton and a congregation that attended Holy Communion once a month. Services continued until September 1970.

Apparently the building itself was mainly of wood with a brick store attached. There was also at one time an old wooden warehouse here which spanned the canal from bank to bank. Both wooden structures have now gone but the brick store still remains, although boarded up. There is a line drawing in *Narrow Boat* by R.C. Rolt that shows the old wooden warehouse stretching over the canal.

This brick store is all that remains of the Barbridge Mission.

WARDLE

Wardle Castle

On a map of Wardle in the Cheshire Record Office, dated 1767 and drawn by Richard Evans of Winsford for the Earl of Dysart, there is shown a large field to the north of Wardle Hall and Broad Lane (now called Green Lane) called Castle Hill. This field name suggests that there was a castle here at one time. The topography, however, does not reinforce this suggestion as the ground here is extremely flat.

RAF Calveley

This Royal Air Force base was built originally in 1940 as an operational fighter station to provide protection from German bombers for the local cities of Liverpool and Manchester. By the end of 1941, Hitler's attentions had been diverted to the Russian front and the threat of bombing the two cities receded. Consequently, the role of RAF Calveley changed to providing advanced fighter training, which it continued to do for the rest of the Second World War. According to Robert Truman on his website www.controltowers.co.uk, it was the Relief Landing Ground for RAF Ternhill with No. 5 (Pilot) Advanced Flying Unit operating Miles Masters from March 1942 to May 1943. This was followed by No 17. (Pilot) AFU, transferred from RAF Watton and RAF Bodney, until the end of January 1944 when the squadron disbanded. Immediately afterwards No. 11 (Pilot) AFU moved here with Oxfords from RAF Shawbury. It was later equipped with Masters then Ansons, Harvards and Hurricanes. The squadron disbanded here in June 1945. The station then became No. 5 Aircrew Holding Unit until October 1945 when No. 22 Service Flying Training School were formed here with Harvards. In May 1946 the Flying Training School moved to RAF Ouston and the airfield finally closed in October 1946.

There is a reference to Sergeant Hugh Clark, Student Pilot at RAF Calveley, provided by his grandson, Martin, on a website referring to RAF Calveley. Apparently Sgt Clark had been posted to No. 5 (P)AFU to fly the Miles Master aircraft, arriving at RAF Ternhill on 4th October 1942. The Masters had been moved out to the Relief Landing Ground at Calveley in May 1942 and so Sgt Clark arrived at Calveley on 14th October. On the night of 16th October, Sgt Clark lost control of his Master at 300 feet while night flying. The aircraft crashed onto the airfield at Calveley, injuring both Sgt. Clark and his instructor. He was hospitalised for a short time but returned to flying on 10th November 1942, and completed his flying training successfully at the beginning of December. After learning to fly the Spitfire, he went on to fly from various RAF stations both in the UK and abroad in countries including India, Saudia Arabia, Palestine, Egypt, Sardinia, France and Germany, before returning to the UK to be demobbed in 1946.

In *Bunbury* edited by Frank Latham and published in 1989, the last known visit by an aeroplane is mentioned, when a Spitfire force-landed after engine failure. The three runways, in a typical triangular form, were broken up but still some traces remain. The associated buildings, however, are still remarkably intact although now being somewhat encroached upon by the light industry estate close by. Most of the buildings have survived because of their agricultural use and even the control tower still stands. It is considered to be the most complete World War Two RAF airfield in Cheshire.

The Control Tower of RAF Calveley as it is today, in remarkably good condition. Behind on the left is the Instructional and Operations Room. On the right are the Floodlight Trailer and Tractor Shed and Fire Tender Shelter.

Park House and Sparrow House, Green Lane

On the enclosed Bryant Map of 1831 the two houses are clearly shown. There are no traces of either of them now, perhaps not surprisingly as they would have been directly affected by the construction of the airfield at RAF Calveley.

CALVELEY

United Dairies Calveley

There is a paragraph referring to this dairy in *Surrounding Districts of Tarporley*, written by Lance Ledward and published in 1993.

"The United Dairies employed a lot of people from surrounding areas. Mr Allan Whalley was the area manager, Tom Stokes was the manager and Mr Eric Manaton was the transport manager. Milk was collected daily from local farms. Milk was sent daily to United Dairies Wood Lane and Willesden by railway tanks. A special train ran daily to bring empty milk tanks and return with loaded ones. Van loads of ten gallon churns were put into railway vans to various destinations along the North Wales coast and Lancashire. Charles Hayes used to drive the milk lorry from the dairy to the station with the milk. This was during the 1939–45 War. The Dairy closed in 1965 along with the station."

A housing estate is now built on this site.

A photograph of United Dairies, Calveley taken in the 1950s.

Calveley Hall

In de Figuerido and Treuherz there is short paragraph concerning Calveley Hall:

"The half-timbered Old Hall, surrounded by a wall with arrow slits, was demolished *c.*1800, but it seems that the Davenport family had long since moved to another timber house which had been encased in brick and then in the 19th century, half-timbered again. When this house was demolished earlier this century, panelling from it was salvaged. Some is at Rookery Hall, Worleston, and some was used to line the smoke room of the Ellerman liner, *City of Durban*. A Georgian carved wood fireplace was also saved and is now in the state dressing room at Capesthorne, another Davenport house. Nothing remains on site, apart from a lodge, a school and other estate buildings."

An early photograph of Calveley Hall.

It is known that the hall was a very popular venue for the hunting fraternity, particularly around the beginning of the twentieth century when fox hunting was in its heyday. Indeed, Mr W.M. Midwood, one of the last owners, was a Master of the Chehire Hunt. In the early 1950s, when it was being put up for sale by the then owners, Bootle Corporation, the *Nantwich Chronicle* sent a reporter to the hall to view it, and the subsequent article proves of some interest. It seems to have been a favourite Cheshire venue, together with Oulton Hall, for the hunting establishment with crowds of 600 to 700 being mentioned. The central Elizabethan core of the building was the most interesting with a magnificent oak-panelled dining room. The morning room was similarly extensively panelled and featured an artistic draping in softwood around a large oil painting over the fireplace. Upstairs in one of the 20 bedrooms there was an outstanding piece of timberwork which is technically described as cusped lozenge in square framing and produces an overall circular pattern. This design is consistent with timber framing on the outside of Elizabethan buildings and suggests an earlier outside wall. Downstairs, there was a beautifully panelled ballroom that had been added to the Hall by

Lord Grosvenor (the first Duke of Westminster). This had a massive central fireplace with two hearths and the smooth wooden floor of maple shining with a high polish.

The interior had previously been affected by dry rot but Bootle Corporation had effectively treated it. It had stood empty for five years since they bought it.

Previous occupiers had been Lord Grosvenor, Capt. Kennedy, Mr Herbert Peel, Mr de Pennefather, Capt. De Knoop, and then Mr W.M. Midwood before Bootle Corporation.

The Hall seems to have been demolished in the early 1950s but the surrounding buildings, including stables and a church, still survive.

ASTON JUXTA MONDRUM

Brayne's Weir

The weir on the River Weaver called Brayne's Weir suggests that there may well have been a mediaeval mill here at one time. There are no traces now.

Worleston National School, Church Road

The first Worleston school called Worleston National School was built in 1852 opposite the end of Baron's Road, Worleston, and in between St Oswald's Church and Church Cottage. It was endowed by the Tomkinson family of Reaseheath Hall and its aim was to provide education for the children in the rural communities of Worleston, Poole, Cholmondeston and Aston juxta Mondrum. It was designed to accommodate 20 in the infant class and 50 in the older classes. This building proved too small for the growing population in later years and so a larger school was built opposite in 1887 and the old school was demolished.

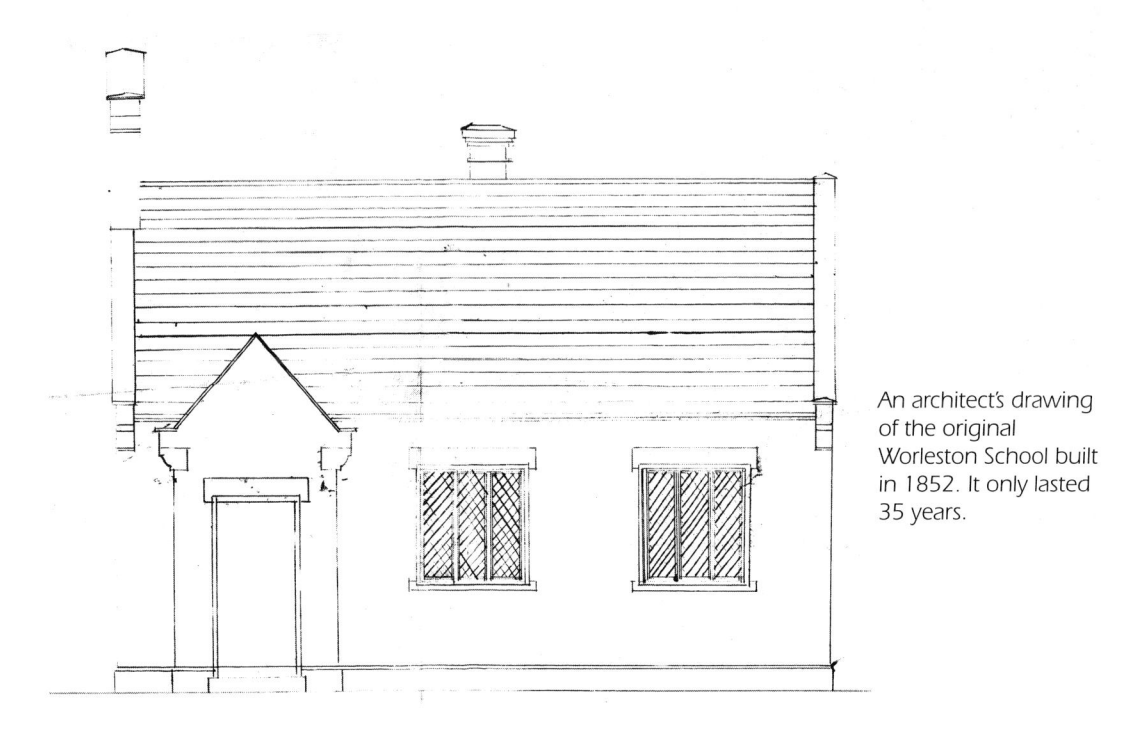

An architect's drawing of the original Worleston School built in 1852. It only lasted 35 years.

Aston juxta Mondrum Windmill

On the Tithe Map of 1842 there is a field called Windmill Croft suggesting that a windmill stood here at one time. The site would be just to the west of Rosefield House but the ground is somewhat flat around here.

The Gate and Hatch, Aston Grove Farm

On the enclosed Bryant Map of 1831, The Gate and Hatch is clearly marked on the main road at Aston Grove Farm. This was clearly a public house then although there is no mention of it as a licensed premises in MacGregor.

CHURCH MINSHULL

An early photgraph showing a thatched Primrose Cottage at Wade's Green, Church Minshull.

The same view as it is now.

Primrose Cottage, Wade's Green

There is an early photograph taken probably at the beginning of the twentieth century showing Primrose Cottage as a small thatched cottage on the main road near Wade's Green. The house has been extensively rebuilt and there are no exterior traces of its earlier origins.

The Cottage

A small thatched black and white cottage stood back from the road where The Cottage stands now. It was demolished around the beginning of the twentieth century when the above-named house was built.

Black and White Cottage

Just to the south of The Badger stood a larger black and white cottage on the roadside. This L-shaped cottage had square panelling three panels high and a tiled roof. It is thought to have been demolished when the four bungalows called The Homesteads were built further back from the road in the 1950s.

An early photograph of Church Minshull showing two black and white cottages on the left and Muslin Row on the right, all of which have gone.

North-West

A later photograph of the same view.

This picture shows the five cottages known as Muslin Row. Beyond them is Beech House with the large beech tree after which it was named.

Muslin Row

Opposite The Cottage stood a terrace of five brick-built cottages called Muslin Row. It is not certain why these cottages were so named, but it would seem likely that there was some connection with the cloth trade. An early photograph shows wooden shutters to the downstairs windows. It is thought that the row was demolished in the 1950s and a telephone exchange now stands on the site. It is good to see that the name Muslin Row has been retained.

The Red Lion

In MacGregor there are records of two licensed premises called The Red Lion in Church Minshull at the same time. At The Red Lion 1, the licensees were: John Harding from 1767 to 1775; Ann Harding in 1777; John Pursnett in 1778; Samuel Higginson from 1779 to 1789; Thomas Williams from 1790 to 1813; Samuel Williams from 1814 to 1816; Charles Ryder in 1817; Charles Pinnington in 1818; and Robert Taylor from 1819 to 1820. Until 1786, The Red Lion 1 had displayed no sign. At The Red Lion 2, the licensee may have been James Major in 1749; it was John Eyres from 1765 to 1779 and Charles Wood from 1782 to 1786. Although it is not known for sure where these public houses were, it is known that Village Farm had been an inn and similarly Church Farm.

Salt Packing Centre

Just to the south of Church Minshull school, on the site of a private house called Sunnyside, stood a Salt Packing Centre. Salt was apparently despatched to all parts of the world from here. This building was destroyed by fire some time ago. The present building was constructed and it became the local Post Office and Stores before conversion to a private house.

Church Minshull Mills

There is evidence that at one time there were two mills in Church Minshull and one was somewhere near Old Hoolgrave on the River Weaver. The other was on a tributary of the Weaver near Minshull Hall. The Tithe Map of 1838 shows Great Mill Field, Little Mill Field and Pool Field here.

However, the present mill at Church Minshull on the River Weaver is thought to be over 600 years old. The adjacent black and white Mill House is dated 1697. The mill has an interesting history and unusually two undershot mill wheels side by side. The east wheel was used to drive the grinding stones for animal feed and the other on the east was used to produce corn flour for human consumption. In the 1930s the east wheel was connected to a generator which produced electricity for the whole of the village. Both mills were in use until floods loosened masonry and jammed the wheels in 1954. There is an evocative description of the mill in the 1940s in Rolt.

Church Minshull Mill. This supplied electricity for the village in the 1940s.

The two mill wheels at Church Minshull. Unusually they stood side by side. The left one drove the machinery for milling corn while the right hand one was for animal foods.

Holly Tree Cottages, Over Road

Two picturesque thatched cottages stood opposite Minshull Hall Gates on the Over road out of Church Minshull. They were still standing in 1922 when they were put up for sale as part of the Ashbrook Towers Estate. One consisted of a kitchen, back kitchen and two bedrooms and the other was described as containing a living room, kitchen, pantry and bedroom, this latter cottage being unoccupied at that time. A modern house called The Hollies stands near where these cottages were.

Ashbrook Towers, Lea Green

It is known that Ashbrook Towers began life as Ashbrook Hall, built around 1870 by Henry Brooke, Esq. who had inherited the lordship of the manor of Church Minshull from his ancestor Sir Richard Brooke, Bart. Henry Brooke, Esq. died on 3rd January 1884 aged 87 years and it is thought that he was succeeded by his son Charles Luxmoore Brooke, late Captain of the 37th Regiment, but he died soon after on 8th January 1890, aged 65. It is thought that he was succeeded by Charles Frederick Coryndon Luxmoore and it is known that Ashbrook Hall had been renamed Ashbrook Towers by 1902. In 1904, there is a report in the *Over Parish Church Magazine* of a fete held here on behalf of the Church Minshull Friendly Society. During the afternoon, the Winsford Temperance Silver Band provided music but the highlight of the afternoon was a balloon ascent and parachute descent by Professor Spencer watched by nearly a thousand people. He ascended rapidly to 2,000 feet, released his hold on the balloon, and sailed gently down to earth as his parachute rapidly deployed, landing safely in a neighbouring field.

Ashbrook Towers, demolished in the 1930s.

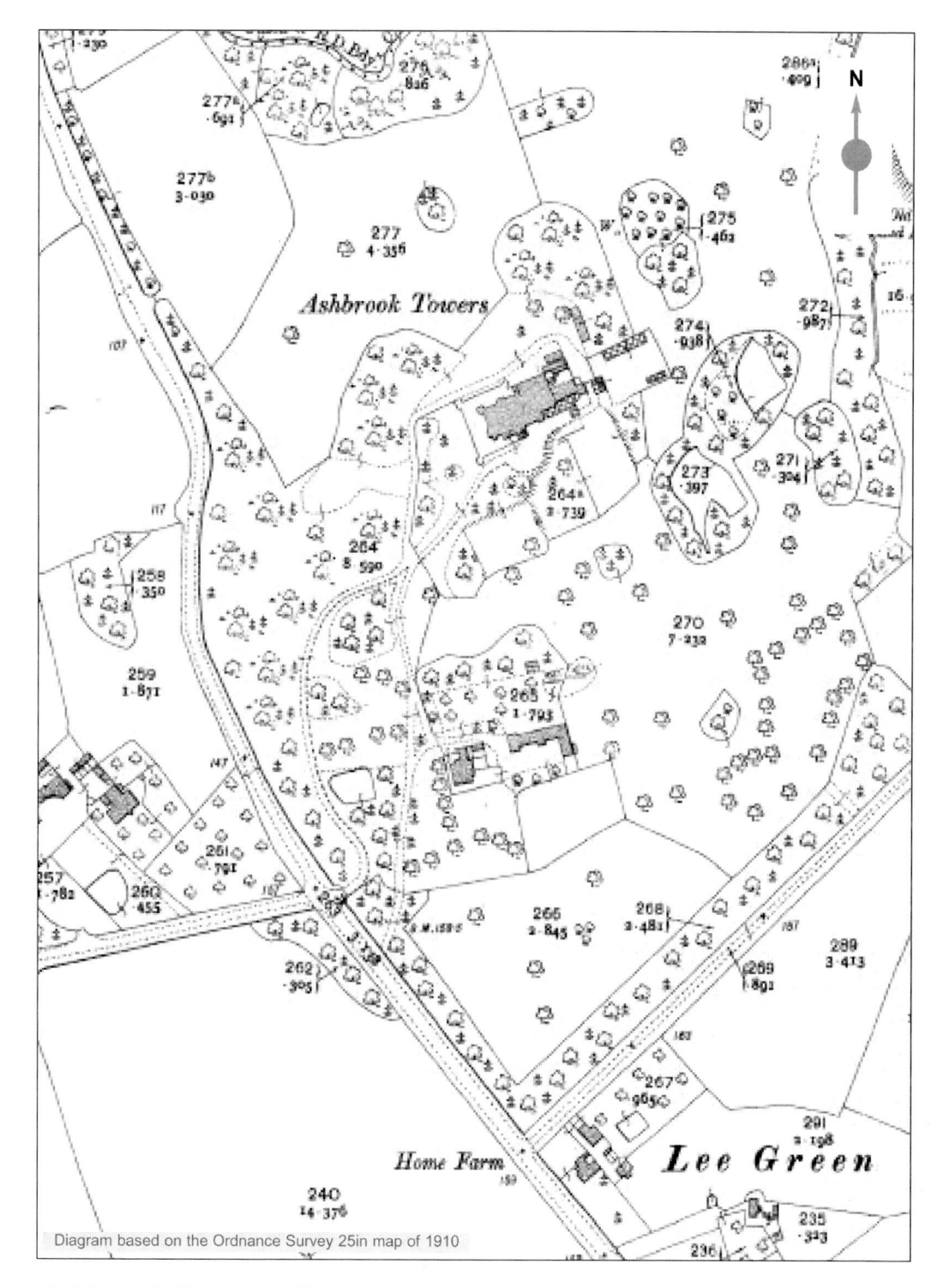

North-West

Ashbrook Towers, Church Minshull

Ashbrook Towers from the side.

In 1922, presumably on the death of Charles Luxmoore, the Ashbrook Estate was put up for sale and the sales particulars are of some interest. Ashbrook Towers is described as:

"A distinctive Country Residence … comprising an area of 53 acres … the moderate-sized Mansion is pleasantly placed in the centre of an Ornamentally Timbered Park, IN THE HEART OF A FAMOUS AGRICULTURAL AND SPORTING COUNTY, hunted by the Cheshire Hounds, whose kennels are not far distant. It is approached from the Worleston to Over and Winsford Main Road by two Drives, the principal of which is marked by a PAIR OF HANDSOME ENTRANCE GATES and which continues through the Shrubberies and Grounds terminating with a broad Carriage Sweep before the Principal Entrance.

"In the Imposing Main Entrance at the base of the Central Tower are, the entrance hall leading to the

"Stately Lounge Hall, 28ft. x 35ft. 9ins. with handsome tiled floor.

"Comfortable Drawing Room, 19ft. x 29ft. (s.w. aspect) with a pleasant projecting recess afforded by the western subsidiary tower.

"A Noble Dining Room, 27ft. 6ins. x 21ft. effectively oak panelled.

"A Light and Airy Library, 22ft. x 19ft. with large Bay Window facing South West.

"The Principal Entertaining Rooms and Bedrooms are fitted with elegant Marble Fireplaces.

"The Morning Room (17ft. 6ins. x 20ft. 6ins.) is approached from the Vestibule which communicates with the SIDE ENTRANCE near which is placed the Lavatories.

"THE FIRST FLOOR is reached by a Broad Principal Staircase terminating in a capacious landing which forms a FINE BILLIARD ROOM, and over the front entrance, facing south with a large Bay Window is a Sunny Boudoir.

"The Principal Bed and Dressing Rooms are seven in number, there being a well arranged day and night nursery on the first floor, also Bathroom and W.C.

"Approached by a Secondary Staircase are Governess' Room and Bedroom, Housemaid's

Pantry, 3 Bedrooms on Second Floor, and two Men's Bedrooms with separate Staircase.

"The Commodious Domestic Apartments include: Business Room, Strong Room, Butler's Pantry, Servants' Hall, Chins Cupboards, Kitchen, Pantry, Dairy, Larder. Scullery, W.C.

"Good Cellars.

"The Outer Offices comprise: Bakehouse, Boothouse, Pottingshed, Mushroom House, Milkhouse and Coalhouse, W.C.

"The Stabling is compact and arranged on either side the Clock Tower, it comprises: Stabling for seven horses with Loosebox and Lofts, Saddleroom, two Looseboxes.

"Garage for 3 Cars and a three-stalled shippon."

There follow descriptions of various buildings within the grounds including the engine house, a pair of cottages, and two sets of kennels. The grounds are described as containing conifers, pines and flowering shrubs with terraced lawns, a croquet lawn and tennis courts. The greenhouses include two peach houses on a southern wall and a conservatory and there is also a partly walled-in kitchen garden.

The Sales Brochure also describes various properties belonging to the estate including The Badger Inn, in the village of Church Minshull, some of which, because they are not named, are difficult to identify.

There is also a later Sales Brochure of $c.1933$ similar to the one mentioned above. It is known that after this sale, the house was dismantled and many fine pieces of furniture and fittings sold, much finding its way abroad, with some going to America.

Appendix

The following photographs (and one line drawing) of houses no longer in Nantwich have come to light since the publication of Lost Houses in Nantwich and they were considered important enough to include in this following edition.

The two authors signing copies of *Lost Houses in Nantwich* at Nantwich Bookshop. October 2005.

A delightful line drawing by John Haydn Jones of the cottage at Kingsley Fields, Nantwich. It stood beyond the old cricket pitch>

A photograph taken around 1913 showing Walter and Caroline Davies outside the bungalow in the garden behind Townsend House, Welsh Row, Nantwich.

A photograph taken in the 1950s showing the latest fashions outside Hilditch's shoe shop at the lower end of High Street, Nantwich.

Appendix

An aerial view of part of Nantwich taken in 1953. It shows the houses in the Snowhill and Swinemarket area before they were demolished. In the centre left is "the old lock-ups" and the filter beds to the right, with the house where Peter Clough lived behind, backing onto the river. In the foreground are houses in Swine Market.

A painting of The White Lion, Swinemarket in 1905.

Lost Buildings around Nantwich

The Carnival procession in 1966 in Beam Street, Nantwich showing some of the cottages in the background which have since been demolished.

Heathbank, off Birchin Lane, Nantwich, the home of Dr and Mrs Hugh Blacklay.

Appendix

Another view of Heathbank. The corner of Heathbank Cottages can just be seen on the right.

Another view of the black and white cottages near the end of Welsh Row, in the rain, and virtually deserted.

BIBLIOGRAPHY

Antiquarian Society of Lancashire and Cheshire Transactions
Awty, B, 'The Charcoal Ironmasters of Cheshire and Lancashire 1600–1785' in
    The Transactions of the Historical Society of Lancashire and Cheshirea Vol. 109, 1957
Cheshire Genealogist
Cheshire History
Cheshire Trade Directories, 1789 onward
Crewe and Shrewsbury Passengers' Association Newsletter
De Figuerido, P, and Treuherz, J, *Cheshire Country Houses*, 1988
Deesider
Dodgson, J McN, *The Placenames of Cheshire*, Pt.3: Nantwich Hundred, 1971
Griffin, A, *Berkeley Towers Crewe: A Short History*, 1993
Hall, J, *The History of Nantwich*, 1883
Historical Society of Lancashire and Cheshire Transactions
Hughes, D, *The Brine Baths Hotel, Nantwich*, 1994
Latham, FA (Ed.), *Acton*, 1995
Latham, FA (Ed.), *Alpraham*, 1969
Latham, FA (Ed.), *Audlem*, 1997
Latham, FA (Ed.), *Bunbury*, 1989
Latham, FA (Ed.), *Wrenbury and Marbury*, 1999
Latham, FA (Ed.), *Wybunbury*, 2003
Ledward, L, *Surrounding Districts of Tarporley*, 1993
MacGregor, Dr AJ, *The Alehouses and Alehousekeepers of Cheshire 1692-1829*, 1992
Mercer, E, *English Vernacular Houses*, 1975
Nantwich Chronicle
Norris, H, 'The Water Powered Corn Mills of Cheshire' in
    The Transactions of the Historical Society of Lancashire and Cheshire, 1965-1966
Nulty, G, *Shavington: The Story of a South Cheshire Village*, 1959
Ormerod, G, *History of Cheshire*, (2nd Ed.) 1882
Richards, R, *Old Cheshire Churches*, (2nd Ed.) 1972
Riley, G, *Ancient Water Wheels on Checkley Brook*, 1987
Rolt, RTC, *Narrow Boat* 1947
Roundabout – a Magazine for Wistaston People
Sedgwick N, *Wistaston: A History of the Parish and Church*, 1960
Yate, B, *By Great Western to Crewe*, 2005

Index

A
Acton 101
alehouse 21, 58, 74, 76
Ashbrook Towers 7, 128, 130
Aston Juxta Mondrum 121, 122
Austerson 42, 65
Austerson Old Hall 7, 65, 66

B
Baddiley 100
Baddiley Church 100, 101
Baddington 41, 73
Barbridge Mission 116
Batherton 10, 41
Batherton Mill 41, 42
Beam Heath 21
beerhouse 35, 36, 73, 74, 75, 76
Berkeley Towers 18
Black Horse 44
Blakelow Chapel 43
Blakenhall 54
Boote's Dye Mill 14
Bridgemere 57
Bridgemere Nurseries 58
Brindley 110
Buckley Mill 10, 11
Burland 106
Burland Castle 107
Burland Farm 107

C
Calveley 119
Calveley Hall 7, 120
Checkley 54
Checkley Green 54
Checkley Hall 54
Checkley Mill 54
Cholmondeley family 73
Chorley 107
Chorley Hall 107
Chorley Water Mill 107
Church Minshull 122, 123, 124, 126, 127, 128, 131
Church Minshull Mills 126

Cock o' Burland 106
Cock o' Poole Hill 115
Coole Pilate 71
Coole Pilate Halt 72

D
Delves Broughton 40
Doddington 54
Doddington Camp 55, 56
Doddington Forge 56
Doddington Mill 57

E
Edleston 73, 74

F
Faddiley 110

G
Grosvenor, Lord 121

H
Hankelow 62, 79
Hatherton 59, 60, 61
hearse house 45, 46, 92
Horse and Jockey 21, 35, 36
Hunsterson 58
Hurleston 114, 115

L
Lea 52
Lea Forge 52, 56

M
Methodist Chapels 11, 23, 24, 28, 78, 100, 116
Mission Church 24

N
Nantwich Middlewich Turnpike Trust 11
Newhall 78
Newhall Castle 79
Newhall Cross 85
Newhall Dairies 80, 81, 82, 83, 84

P
Peacock Inn 24
Poole 115, 121

R
RAF Calveley 117, 118, 119
RAF Hack Green 6, 66, 67, 69, 70, 72
Railway Stations 10, 87, 88, 89, 114
Ravensmoor 76, 77, 78, 100
Reaseheath 111, 112
Rockwood Inn 13
Rookery Hall 10, 112, 114, 120
Rope 22

S
Schroeder, Barron von 10
Shavington 26
Shavington Mill 26, 27
Sheppenhall Hall 78, 79
Smallpox Hospital 77, 78
Sound 75
St Chads Wybunbury 47
St.Chad's Church 45
Stapeley 33, 39, 40
Stapeley Mill 39
Stoke 116

T
tollhouses 11, 15, 25, 26, 38, 59, 116
Trufood Ltd 89

U
United Dairies 80, 119

W
Walgherton 49, 50, 51, 61
Wardle 116, 117
watermills 49, 54, 79, 115
Wells Green Farmhouse 19, 20
Wheelock Turnpike Trust 15
Wilbraham, Lady 110
Willaston 7, 23, 24, 25, 26
windmills 49, 50, 79, 100, 122
Wistaston 11, 12, 14, 18, 19, 21, 24
Wistaston Mill 11, 15, 16, 17
Wolfe's Cottage 29, 30
Woolstanwood 10, 11
Worleston 10, 112, 113, 120, 121
Wrenbury 87, 89, 100
Wrenbury Green 90, 91, 92, 93
Wybunbury 7, 43, 44, 47, 48, 61
Wybunbury Mill 48